ADVANCE PRAISE FOR
NO PERFECT LOVE

"This book has the potential to change lives and heal relationships. Couples can benefit from their first date through every stage of their relationship."

> – Dr. Drew Pinsky, nationally known doctor, NY Times Best-selling Author and media personality, host of 7 television shows

"*No Perfect Love* is just about the perfect self-help relationship book! Of the short non-fiction books we've come by in 2022, this is certainly one of the best! There's just something about how Dr. Alyson Nerenberg is able to take things as mundane as case studies and make them so interesting and compelling. This book is short yet dense. There are lessons to be learned at every flip of the page. There's hardly any wasted space in this whole book. Everything is either insightful, interesting, and/or useful to the reader. And that's probably the books greatest strength: it's shear usefulness and practicality. We really believe this book can change lives. It can save relationships. It can save marriages. It can keep families together. Those are huge stakes and implications. There is tremendous value on every page."

> – Outstanding Award Creator Committee's Review

"*No Perfect Love* is an incredibly worthwhile book for therapists and the general public, written by one of the leaders in our field who has been involved for over three decades. Dr. Alyson Nerenberg shares "insider information" in terms of what it is like to be a therapist and to be a client. It is a very enjoyable read that makes human the therapy experience so all of us can be helped by realizing that it is a myth that the process always works in some magical way. Dr. Nerenberg is a beacon in the psychology field and her book will help guide anyone struggling with a challenging relationship."

– Ralph Earle, MDiv, Ph.D., ABPP, LMFT, CSAT, past president
of the American Association for Marriage and Family Therapy, author
of *Lonely All the Time* and *Conversations: Therapy and Spiritual Growth*

"If you are hoping to find the perfect love—as so many people are—or are disappointed to realize that your marriage or relationship is not perfect, then *No Perfect Love* is the perfect book for you! Written in a very engaging style and filled with the stories of many people, and with multiple exercises and suggestions for dealing with your own or your partner's unrealistic expectations, perfectionism, or narcissism, you will find this book extremely helpful. Psychologist Dr. Nerenberg is a very experienced couples therapist and I highly recommend her book."

— Jennifer Schneider, M.D., Ph.D., author of *Back from Betrayal:
Recovering from the Trauma of Infidelity* and *Disclosing Secrets*

"With *No Perfect Love*, Dr. Alyson Nerenberg has shattered the myth of 'happily ever after,' moving couples from Disney princess pipe dreams into the real world, where even the best of relationships is far from perfect. Her no nonsense take on relationships and how to thrive in them, despite their many flaws, is rock solid. My professional experience of Dr. Nerenberg is one of integrity, wit, and insight. This book carries those gifts into useful words of wisdom."

— Robert Weiss, Ph.D, author of *Out of the Doghouse*
and *Prodependence: The End of Codependency*

"Dr. Nerenberg dispels, once and for all, the myth that if a relationship is right, our partner and others will automatically know what we want and need without ever asking. This is a relationship-promoting, life-enhancing, divorce-busting how-to book for creating and sustaining healthy long-term relationships. I highly recommend it."

– Dr. Helen Friedman, clinical psychologist, award-winning radio
show host of *Psych Talk*, associate clinical professor
at The Saint Louis University School of Medicine,
past president of the St. Louis Psychological Association

"Healthy relationships, formed by trust, respect, communication, and understanding, are the basis of society and a source of both joy and love. Dr. Nerenberg, through her personal wisdom and clinical experience, helps couples navigate the challenges of these fundamental requirements. She addresses the inevitable personal disappointments and emotional pain that characterize most, if not all, long-term relationships. And she does so with an openness and perspective that leaves the reader with a strong sense of direction and hope."

– Dr. Brian F. Shaw, one of the originators
of applied cognitive-behavior therapy (CBT) for clinical practice,
principal of Brian Shaw Psychology Professional Corporation,
CEO, Continicare Corporation.

"Dr. Nerenberg's 30 years of clinical wisdom shines on every page of *No Perfect Love*. A timely and fresh look at the connection between narcissism and the striving for perfection, *No Perfect Love* takes the reader on a compassionate, at times personal, and practical journey to heal from the narcissistic drum beat that demands perfection in order to be loved. Covering a wide range of topics including romance, parenting, athletics, and the culture at large, *No Perfect Love* is a welcome road map of relief and insight that points to the need for it to be on everyone's bookshelf."

— Kenneth M. Adams, Ph.D., author of *Silently Seduced*
and *When He's Married to Mom*

"In sync with the current cultural pressure of perfectionism, *No Perfect Love* dismantles the 'Happily Ever After' myth and transforms it into reality delivering the reader into gratitude for the life they have. Dr. Nerenberg expertly reminds us about what it's really like to be in a relationship. Whether with a spouse, children, or parents, the reader is guided to examine their patterns and their inner workings of what it takes to love, lose, and fight for our truth. *No Perfect Love* is a book worth reading and a journey worth taking!"

– Alexandra Katehakis, Ph.D., author, *Mirror of Intimacy: Daily Reflections on Emotional and Erotic Intelligence*

"Dr. Alyson Nerenberg wrote a truly outstanding book in which she tackles the toxic, omnipresent cultural pull of perfection in relationships head-on, supporting the reader in facing imperfections directly and effectively. The exercises at the end of each chapter guide the reader in delving into the obstacles that a perfection-based orientation promote and in courageously working around them. Her clinical examples bring her expertly explained concepts to life and her personal anecdotes make her entirely relatable as someone who doesn't just work with others who struggle with imperfections, but someone who shares her own as well. This is a tremendous new resource that we will absolutely be using with our clients!"

– Drs. Bill and Ginger Bercaw, clinical psychologists, certified sex addiction therapists, certified sex therapists, authors of *The Couple's Guide to Intimacy*

"Dr. Nerenberg uses her skilled knowledge as one of the most sought-after individual and couples psychologists in Philadelphia to provide the reader with profound insight that is both down-to-earth and applicable. The reality is that few people at some time in their life are not impacted by the insidious roadblock of perfectionism.

The information she provides is clear, relevant, and caring in its discussions and explanations that readers can easily apply to their own life experiences. Nerenberg's examples throughout the book, based on her clients' progress, provide insight, practical information, and, for many, hope for their own movement forward. For those readers who apply the wisdom in the book to their own life, Dr. Nerenberg provides useful exercises and journal prompts and questions for additional thought. This is the kind of book that will remain applicable to a reader for years to come."

— Jeanne Stanley, Ph.D., Watershed Counseling & Consultation Services, author of *Teaching LGBTQ Psychology*

"If you are experiencing any type of challenges in your relationships, from family, to friends to work, this is a must read for you. Dr. Alyson Nerenberg approaches the delicate subject of love and relationships with laudable expertise...She takes readers through an array of anecdotes personal and therapeutic advice, research data...(and) includes exercises for self reflection and evaluation. I liked how Dr. Nerenberg boldly and candidly addresses various issues in her book, one of them being the issue of generational trauma. This is one of the major causes of relationship failures because it greatly shapes or alters a person's opinions, character and emotional capacity. I learned about the Karpman Drama Triangle, and how people unconsciously played different roles in it. She also elaborates on self empathy, forgiveness, gratitude, boundaries, and more...I loved the book. It's very educative and life changing."

— Keith Abuja, 5 Stars, Readers Favorite

Publisher's Cataloguing-In-Publication Data
Nerenberg, Alyson
No Perfect Love: Shattering the Illusion of Flawless Relationships

ISBN: 978-1-7349563-7-5

Printed in the United States of America

First Edition

Editor/Publisher: Joy E. Stocke/Raquel B. Pidal
Editor: Vincent Allen
Copyeditor: Londyn Korol
Design and Composition: Tim Ogline / Ogline Design

Published by Tree of Life Books
PO Box 81
557 Rosemont-Ringoes Rd
Sergeantsville, New Jersey 08557

www.treeoflifetreeofjoy.com

NO PERFECT LOVE

SHATTERING THE ILLUSION OF FLAWLESS RELATIONSHIPS

Alyson Nerenberg, Psy. D.

Tree
of Life
Books

"Just because you are happy
it does not mean that the day is perfect
but that you have looked beyond its imperfections."

– Bob Marley

*This book is dedicated like everything I do
and everything I am to my family and favorite people:
Jeffrey, Amanda, Marissa and Justin Nerenberg,
as well as my favorite fluffy white dog, Rosie.*

TABLE OF CONTENTS

INTRODUCTION

WELCOME!

I'm so glad you picked up this book and have decided to embark on an incredible journey to heal your relationship! As you begin reading, I want to clarify that this is more than a self-help guide, it's a love story dedicated to my patients and you. Most important, it's a celebration of the resiliency that lives within all of us.

The premise is simple: Regardless of what social media posts display, together we will dismantle the illusion that relationships are perfect. In fact, in all important relationships, especially romantic relationships, there are disappointments and struggles. Here's the good news, when we work through the difficulties in our primary romantic partnerships —the times when we're confronted with both our and our partner's character defects —we both grow. Not only do we grow, we thrive. Acknowledging our own and our significant other's vulnerabilities and shortcomings makes us human and makes our relationships stronger.

PERFECTLY IMPERFECT

In the past thirty years, I have seen thousands of individuals and couples suffering from relationship problems. I have laughed with them. I have cried with them. I have learned from them all. In my therapy practice, I have had the incredible opportunity to help my patients transform their pain into power and, in doing so, I have been awed by their courage and inspired by their resiliency.

My patients have allowed me to walk beside them as they shared their stories and together, we worked intensely to change their narratives and create more love in their lives. Throughout this process, not only have my patients grown but I have grown too. I describe my patients' life lessons along with my own. I use psychological theory as well as 12-step philosophies and popular culture references in order to illustrate all of our life-changing journeys as we shatter our illusions of perfect relationships in order to become more real and authentic in our acceptance of life's fragilities.

Although 12-step philosophies have often been associated with Alcoholics Anonymous, I believe that many of the strategies and slogans can be expanded to provide wisdom for us all. In this book, I share many of the principles I use to counsel patients in order to make sense of the struggles we all face. For example, in writing this book I have my own fear of being exposed and putting my stories out there. To alleviate my own anxiety, I remember how often I have said to my patients, "Ninety percent of life is just showing up." This book is my opportunity to "just show up" in a written form. I also frequently quote the 12-step philosophies saying that moving forward in life is a matter of progress, not perfection.

And that is OK. In fact, perfectly imperfect is often the best possible outcome. Consider parenting. The pediatrician and psychoanalyst

Donald Winnicott described the concept of the "good enough parent." He explained that for a child to grow in healthy ways, the child doesn't need a parent who is perfectly attuned and responsive at all times. Instead, the child needs a parent who is showing up, doing his or her best, and meeting most of the child's emotional needs. A perfect parent, because he or she does everything for the child in a perfect way, will actually stunt the child's growth by preventing the child from learning and growing and developing a sense of autonomy and self.

The perfect parent is imperfect. The imperfect parent is perfect.

I have adapted this term —perfectly imperfect —to the whole of my life and especially this book. My goal here is to be a "good enough" student/therapist/author. My challenge in life and in writing this book is to let go of my unrealistically high standards enough to let my visions soar. My goal is to be perfectly imperfect because, with that, you can interpret this book in ways that make sense to you, in ways that help you learn and grow as an individual and a partner.

THE VALUE OF JOURNALING

At the end of each chapter, you will find questions and exercises giving you the opportunity to reflect in meaningful ways about the topics I share with you. Some people choose to buy a journal and write their thoughts on paper, while others prefer their computers, or even their phones. For me, the act of writing down my thoughts in a beautifully decorated journal is helpful. I suggest that if you purchase a notebook or journal, you keep it in a private place so you will have a sacred space to document your growth. No matter what you prefer, the point is to try the exercises, so feel free to choose whatever method works for you. Some of you may not want to journal. That is OK too. In that case, the questions in these pages are here to plant seeds you may want to think about later. Let's begin here with four questions you may already have asked yourself:

How do unrealistic standards hold me back in life?

Do I not start projects because I am afraid that I will fail?

Do I avoid dating because I am only going to be let down?

Do I avoid relationships because of perceived imperfections in myself or others?

1

LIVING IN A CULTURE
OF NARCISSISM
AND PERFECTION

NARCISSISM

Famed psychoanalyst Arnold Rothstein's definition of narcissism is "the unrelenting pursuit of perfection." Consider the following statement as an example: "If only I had the perfect wife, I wouldn't have problems." As you read that statement and apply it to your own life, you should feel free to substitute the word wife with husband, girlfriend, boyfriend, job, children, car, house, paycheck, or whatever else you can think of. And pay attention to the fact that when you pursue perfection in this narcissistic way, you are pushing blame for your shortcomings onto others.

With narcissistic behavior —and, let's face it, we all have some narcissistic traits —there is little accountability and the problem is always with someone else. This does not automatically mean we are bad or defective people. It simply means we are human, and we have room to grow.

From a clinical perspective, true narcissists —individuals diagnosed with Narcissistic Personality Disorder —have an inflated sense of their own importance, an excessive need for admiration, and a lack of empathy for others. They are difficult and unpleasant to deal with, though they can at times seem charming, and they are not easy to treat.

Thankfully, not many people are clinically diagnosed with Narcissistic Personality Disorder. That said, almost everyone, even the most psychologically healthy among us, will at times engage in narcissistic behaviors. We will inflate our sense of self-importance, we will excessively seek admiration, and we will fail to feel empathy for others. And needless to say, these behaviors can, and often do, lead to self-esteem issues and troubled relationships.

Although narcissistic behavior may on the surface look extremely confident, behind the mask, the individual engaging in such behavior typically has a fragile self-esteem —either in the moment or longer-term. As such, that person is vulnerable to even the slightest criticism.

In this respect, narcissistic behavior is a defense mechanism rather than evidence of a somewhat rare personality disorder. This was certainly the case with my client Jordan, whom we will discuss later in this chapter, whose modus operandi in his romantic life seemed to be: I'll find flaws with you and break up with you before you have a chance to find flaws with and break up with me. Narcissistic behavior, but not true narcissism.

PERFECTION

As Rothstein states, narcissism and perfection are often deeply intertwined. One leads to the other, the other leads to the one; our society is rampant with both. To illustrate, let's think about Disney movies.

In our society, children (especially little girls) are raised watching Disney movies. In most of these stories, a beautiful princess overcomes obstacles to find her ideal true love. So basically, these movies teach little girls (and boys) that once they find their Prince (or Princess) Charming, they will ride off into the sunset and have the happy ending they deserve.

As we get older, the same fantasy is promoted by romantic comedies. All the protagonists have to do is work through a few misunderstandings and erroneous beliefs and they will find the ideal partner, the man (or woman) who will provide them with everlasting happiness.

Television is equally to blame. Even in a show like *Sex and The City* about sophisticated Manhattanites, the main characters are all searching for their perfect love. Shows like *The Bachelor* and *The Bachelorette* take things a step further by turning the search for a perfect partner into a competition.

Our culture endlessly promotes the illusion of relationship perfection through movies, TV, and even our use of social media. In today's world, it is not enough for a couple to have a beautiful private moment of getting engaged. Now they must hire a professional photographer, or at least have a friend who is good at taking pictures, show up to document the occasion for Instagram, Facebook, and Snapchat, all of which are platforms where people airbrush their lives to seem incredibly successful and happy.

REALITY

As a psychologist who specializes in couples therapy, I frequently encounter couples who are devastated when the mask of perfection is taken off. Suddenly, they confront the reality that they are married to someone who has deeply disappointed them. Either directly or indirectly, these couples are asking: How do I stay in a relationship with a person who has failed to be perfect? Why should I stay invested in a relationship after I have been deeply hurt, disappointed, and disillusioned?

In many instances, it is easier to just run. Separation and divorce rates have never been higher and the stigma of divorce has significantly decreased. Plus, so many people come from single-parent households that starting over has been modeled through the past generations. These days, separation and divorce are almost the norm. It can be far easier to say, "My relationship is failing," and to blame that failure on the other person than to dig beneath the surface to find, accept, and work with our partner's and *our own* issues.

When a couple walks in the door for counseling, I view them as brave. They are fighting for their relationship by confronting their issues instead of taking the easy way out and quickly running away to avoid more pain. As someone who has the urge to avoid, or at least to sulk when my feelings are hurt, I deeply respect the couples who arrive in my office with their sleeves rolled up, ready to dive into the trenches and work through their heartache.

RUPTURES AND REPAIRS

One of the concepts I often talk about with these couples is my theory of ruptures and repairs. I believe that in every long-term relationship, whether it is a friendship, a familial relationship, a romantic relationship, or even a therapy relationship, there are ruptures and (hopefully) repairs. Ruptures can be disappointments, misunderstandings, or betrayals of trust. Ruptures are inevitable, even in the best of relationships. The question is when ruptures happen, how will we respond?

The difficult work of any relationship is the job of repairing ruptures. Yesterday, in a therapy session, I illustrated this concept by using my own therapeutic relationship with my patient as an example. A few days earlier, a former patient called to say he was having some new struggles in his marriage and wanted some support. I was in a session with another patient when he called, so he left a message. I listened to the message as soon as I could, but I didn't have time to call him back. And then I forgot.

The following day he called again and my first words to him were a sincere apology for not getting back to him sooner. I commended him on his persistence in trying to reach me and we set up an appointment. My not calling him back was a small rupture in our relationship. It could have been viewed as hurtful or insensitive. However, my quick apology for my mistake was the simple repair our relationship needed. And because he knew me and realized the lack of response was out of my character, he quickly forgave me, and we moved on.

This rupture and repair was actually a good thing for our therapeutic relationship and a way for my client to learn by example. First and foremost, I illustrated that making a mistake need not cause a person to go down a shame spiral. I also showed him that if he was willing to show me forgiveness, maybe his spouse would be able to forgive him for his recent violation of their relationship boundaries.

Couples therapy is a great place for repairing the ruptures that happen in every relationship. It can help each partner learn to slow down and listen to the other partner without getting caught in feelings of shame or inadequacy. When we are challenged or criticized, often our first instinct is to defend ourselves profusely. But that instinct does not always serve us. In fact, most of the time it does not. A couples therapy office is a safe place for partners to learn to push aside this first instinct and turn instead to communication skills such as talking and listening with an open mind as well as an open heart. It becomes a space where each partner can learn to develop empathy for the other, and empathy for themselves.

Couples therapy is also a place to learn that although our narcissistic, childlike selves may seek perfect relationships, perfect relationships are not possible. The real value of relationships is not the illusion of perfection but the opportunity to show up, share our vulnerabilities, hurts, and character defects, and be seen and appreciated for who we are.

THE NARCISSISTIC/PERFECTIONISTIC EXPECTATIONS WE PUT ON OUR CHILDREN

In March of 2019, many of us were outraged when the story broke that two famous actresses, Lori Loughlin and Felicity Huffman, bypassed their children's college admission process. Basically, Loughlin and Hoffman paid a college admissions coach, William (Rick) Singer, to help their daughters cheat on their SATs and blatantly lie about their credentials so that they would be admitted into prestigious and elite colleges. These actresses were not alone in their participation in Singer's scheme. Dozens of other wealthy parents disregarded the values of honesty and integrity to beat the admissions system.

Our country was fascinated by this scandal as it graced the cover of *People* and countless other publications, was viewed on entertainment news shows, and resulted in a quickly produced Lifetime movie. People could not believe how or why beautiful, wealthy celebrities who seemingly "had it all" would still feel the need to cheat.

To me, one of the most fascinating parts of this scandal was that people were so shocked by these celebrities' willingness to disregard the law to get the outcome they wanted. Throughout our nation, they were vilified as the personification of entitlement.

As a psychologist, my perspective was a bit different. Instead of blaming and judging Loughlin and Huffman (and the others who cheated), I viewed them as a symptom of the rampant narcissism and perfectionism in our culture. For many years, children have been seen by parents as "extensions of themselves." As such, a parent's self-worth is directly tied to their children's success. At the same time, getting accepted into a prestigious college has become more and more difficult.

The prevailing thought for many parents is: "You are not enough unless your children are extremely successful." I have seen this mindset expand past the classroom into the athletic world. Your worth as a parent is judged by whether your child makes the "travel team." It is not enough for your daughter to take dance classes for fun, she needs to be on a competitive dance team. It is not sufficient for your son to be a member of a club, he needs to be the president.

All of these raised expectations lead us to put pressure on our children, as well as on ourselves. After all, getting your child to travel games, dance practices, and extracurricular activities takes an extreme amount of time and organization. As such, parents are stressed out and become competitive with each other rather than embracing all of their children's successes in the community.

When my oldest daughter was accepted into an Ivy League college, an old friend who I had lost touch with reached out to me and said this was evidence of some "damn good parenting." Although her intent was to be kind and complimentary, it rubbed me the wrong way. I thought, *If my two younger children don't go to schools of that caliber, does that make me any less of a parent?*

Upon reflection, I actually believe the opposite. It is much more challenging to support my youngest child, who has a learning disability, than my oldest, who is wonderfully self-motivated and independent. Attending Individualized Educational Planning (IEP) meetings, learning about ways to support dyslexia, and finding the resources available to help my youngest child were extremely challenging tasks. And my younger daughter's goal in finding a college wasn't to get into the most highly rated college; it was to find the best fit for her.

As parents, we need to be sensitive about the amount of pressure

—motivated by our sense of narcissistic perfection—that we are putting on ourselves and our children. Often, we are not only making our own lives more difficult, we are damaging our children. Teenage depression, anxiety, and suicide rates are extremely high. In fact, according to the 2019 Youth Behavioral Risk Factor Surveillance System, 18.8 percent of high school students have seriously considered attempting suicide and 8.9 percent have actually attempted suicide. These rates are alarmingly high and should be a wakeup call for all of us that we need to quickly change how we are parenting and lessen the expectations we are putting on teenagers. To be frank, life would be a lot better for everyone if we would work together to build up all of the children in our community, not just the athletic and academic superstars. To me, more important than the question, "Where is your child going to school?" is the question, "Is your child being raised with character and good values?"

Hopefully, the college admissions scandal is a wake-up call to both parents and college admissions officers. We need to focus more on our children's capacity for kindness, empathy, and strong character traits, as opposed to putting pressure on them to "look perfect." The narcissistic pursuit of perfection that we continually foist upon them does not serve them —not as kids, not as adults, not as individuals, and certainly not in relationships.

THE NARCISSISTIC/PERFECTIONISTIC EXPECTATIONS WE PUT ON OUR RELATIONSHIPS

Our culture promotes the illusion of looking for the perfect mate not only through movies, TV, and social media, but through the abundance of dating apps where, if you pay a fee, you have the opportunity to meet hundreds of potential partners until you find the ideal match.

Unfortunately, dating apps are a business with the goal of getting users to spend as much time and money as possible. Many of my patients spend hours and hours lost in the "rabbit hole" of trying to find the perfect partner via one app or another (or several at the same time). They become obsessed and lose time and energy they could be spending on their careers or hobbies.

In such cases, part of our work together includes setting boundaries around the amount of time they spend on dating apps, the number of apps they use, and their expectations regarding the individuals they meet on these apps and the relationships they will have with those people. For example, we may set aside 30 minutes each day to check in with dating apps. We might also limit the number of apps the person is using. Most of all, we will focus the individual on developing real connections with real people instead of fantasy connections with airbrushed versions of real people.

Jordan

Jordan is a master of the first date. He has it down to a science. He is a handsome 30-year-old financial analyst with a great haircut and an even better condominium. In fact, from the top of his high-rise you can see a view of Philadelphia all the way to Independence Hall, which happens to be a part of his dating ritual. He meets attractive women on dating apps like Bumble or Hinge and begins an easy banter with them about television shows and music. His strategy is to keep it light and funny. His sense of humor is great, and he can be both witty and charming. After several days of talking, he makes plans to meet his latest date for dinner. He meets her at a trendy restaurant and then takes her back to the roof of his building to show her the panoramic view. Often, these evenings culminate in sex back in his apartment.

Sometimes Jordan calls the women again, but often he doesn't. Instead, he finds perceived flaws: one of them laughs too loud, another speaks with an accent, another is a vegetarian. Jordan calls their flaws "deal breakers" and can't envision himself living a life with a "less than perfect" partner.

The problem with this pattern of behavior is that Jordan is desperately lonely. He avoids intimacy but complains that he is extremely isolated and miserable. Worse still, none of these women ever gets to know the real Jordan —a recovering alcoholic who, despite his polished appearance, believes he is socially awkward and unlovable.

For the most part, Jordan's low self-image is the result of childhood trauma. His mother was cold and rejecting, which taught him that he was not deserving of love and acceptance and that others would never willingly or fully meet his needs for connection, intimacy, and love. As an adult, pushing away any possibility of genuine connections has become Jordan's maladaptive attempt to protect himself. Basically, he will reject a woman before she can reject him.

In therapy, I often reference popular culture with my patients, sometimes by discussing TV shows and movies to reinforce my perspective. This strategy worked with Jordan, who was also a TV and movie buff. I compared him to Jerry Seinfeld, who broke up with women for reasons like being a "close talker" or a "double-dipper." Jordan could not help but laugh at the comparison.

After we connected over our common love of *Seinfeld*, I went a little deeper and brought up one of my favorite movies: *Good Will Hunting*. I asked Jordan if he remembered the scene where Will, played by Matt Damon, told his therapist, Sean, played by Robin Williams, he was not going to call Minnie Driver's character Skylar again because their date was so perfect. He was afraid of getting to know her on a deeper level and discovering her imperfections.

What Sean explained was that maybe Will was afraid of letting Skylar see his own flaws. Sean then said that what he loved the most about his wife, who had passed away, was her imperfections. That was what made her "uniquely her." He went on to share a humorous memory of how she would fart in her sleep, and how once it was so bad that it even woke up the dog. As Will and Sean both laughed, Sean stated that Skylar was not going to be perfect. Nor was Will. What was magical was how they were going to be together.

The reason Will was avoiding intimacy was that he viewed himself as flawed because he was abused as a child. My patient, Jordan, also viewed himself as flawed, primarily because he'd been neglected as a child. After using popular culture as a gateway to discuss this dilemma, we were able to process and work through the wounds of his childhood and his adult-life issues with trust and vulnerability.

Over time, Jordan began to open up and trust me as his therapist. He was also able to open up and become vulnerable with some of his friends in Alcoholics Anonymous. As this occurred, we began to challenge the cognitive distortions that held him back in his romantic relationships. To that end, I gave him experiments such as tolerating discomfort, going on a second date with a "flawed" human being, and sharing some more personal parts of his own story with the women he dated.

PERFECTION IS BORING AND STAGNANT

Though most of us do not enjoy the "drama" of imperfect relationships, we would likely be bored if we were consistently in agreement with the people around us on every aspect of life and existence. More importantly, we would fail to learn and grow from our differences. Without the occasional imperfection, there would be very little *life* in our lives.

Nevertheless, we pursue perfection, and when we don't achieve it or our relationships don't achieve it, we sometimes choose to cut and run. Like Jordan, we use the flaws of others as an excuse to avoid becoming vulnerable and risking our own flaws being exposed. And then we end up lonely, emotionally isolated, and disconnected from potential intimacy.

To avoid this "permanently solo (even when we're in a relationship)" outcome, we must step away from our need, desire, and expectation of perfection from ourselves, others, and our relationships. We must accept that others are flawed, just as we are, and that our flaws are what make us unique and endearing. At the same time, when we encounter true disagreements, we must view these not as insurmountable obstacles, but as opportunities to know one another better and develop deeper intimacy.

EXERCISE 1:
Examine Your Narcissistic Pursuit of Perfection

Each of us, at times, pursues perfection in narcissistic ways. In so doing, we fail to be accountable for our actions, usually by pushing blame for conflicts, bad behavior, and a lack of connection onto others. The problem, as we see it, is with others. We engage in this tactic to avoid looking at, accepting, and addressing our own shortcomings.

Nowhere is this more evident than in our interpersonal relationships. To examine how this has manifested in your life, create a timeline of your past romantic relationships. When you have all of your relationships listed in chronological order, list the ways in which your desire/need for perfection has impacted each relationship. After you have done this, look for themes that have played out throughout your relationship history.

EXERCISE 2:
Tolerating the Discomfort of Imperfection

This is an exercise I often use with patients who are single and looking to date. I describe the concept of dating as similar to following traffic lights. I ask my patients to describe what their red light, yellow light, and green light behaviors are.

Red light behaviors refer to behaviors that would end the dating relationship. Each person's red lights are different. Examples of legitimate deal-breakers might include:

- If you are in recovery and the other person is actively using illegal drugs.
- The other person is still married or living with an ex.

- The other person is unemployed and living with his or her parents.

Yellow light behaviors are signs that you should proceed with caution. They are not necessarily deal-breakers, but they should encourage you to find out more information over time. Each person's yellow lights are different. Yellow light behaviors might include:

- The other person is recently divorced and still holds on to a lot of resentments toward their ex.
- A healthy lifestyle is important to you, but the other person doesn't exercise regularly or eat healthy food.
- The other person is consistently thirty minutes late and this causes you to feel devalued.

Green light behaviors occur when someone exhibits positive behaviors that you believe are necessary for a healthy relationship. Each person's green lights are different. Examples of green light behaviors might include:

- When the other person says that he or she will call you at a certain time and then does.
- The other person has interests and values similar to your own.
- The other person is available for and seeking the same type of relationship you are seeking.

Create a list of your own red, yellow, and green lights. Compare this list to your past and current relationships —not just romantic relationships, but friendships and other relationships.

EXERCISE 3:
Developing Empathy for Yourself and Others

This simple exercise is a way of beginning to develop compassion and empathy for yourself and your significant other. To begin, find a picture of yourself as a child at the age when you felt most vulnerable. Stare at that picture and remember what it felt like to be that age. Think of the insecurities, struggles, and fears you had to overcome. Stare into that child's eyes and notice his or her expression. Write a paragraph about what life was/is like for this child.

Now spend a moment visualizing your adult-self sending that child kindness, compassion, and love. Write that child a short letter filled with this kindness, compassion, and love.

When you are done, hang that picture and the letter you've written where you will see them frequently. It may be in your office next to your computer or on the mirror in your bathroom. You might even want to frame this picture and letter so you can always have them as a visual reminder of your need to have compassion for the wounded child within.

If you are in a relationship, ask your partner to do this same exercise and to share his or her experience with it. If you feel like it, write a letter to your partner's inner child that is as supportive and loving as the letter you wrote to your own.

2

WHERE DOES ALL OF THIS PERFECTIONISM COME FROM?

Years ago, I went to a training and the speaker said to a room full of psychologists, "Realize that you are not just treating the person sitting on your couch. You are treating her mother too. And her mother's mother. In fact, you are trying to treat generations of trauma by breaking the cycle of behaviors that have often occurred for many years."

MY BACKSTORY

Although I always knew I was fortunate to have a great mother, from an early age I was also aware that she was a worrier. She worried all the time. I knew she loved me deeply, but she was concerned with how I was measuring up. As a stay-at-home mother for many years, her self-worth was connected to how my brother and I were faring. When I was in elementary school and middle school and I had a test, she wouldn't just ask how I did. First, she asked about my friends and their tests saying, "How did Jennifer do? What about Tami?" She was constantly measuring me against others to see if I could keep up. This was not about cruelty or competitiveness on her part. Her own anxiety colored her thoughts, even when she was raising us to the best of her ability.

However, I took this to mean I wasn't good enough or smart enough.

And by the time I reached high school, I rebelled by not trying as hard as I could. I was tired of being judged and compared to others and decided if I couldn't be the "studious one," I might as well become the "social one." My identity became very connected to my friendships and the boys I dated. It wasn't until college, when I was living on my own, that I claimed the truth. I loved to learn and could do so for myself.

My mother was an only child who did not have any siblings to "run things by," so I became her friend, her confidante, and the soother of her anxiety. It was great training ground to become a psychologist. Both of her parents had died by the time she was 36, and she had married my father, who was also an only child and a criminal defense attorney. As my father's professional and financial responsibilities increased, he turned to alcohol to soothe his stress. I responded by becoming a classic "parentified child," helping my mother by giving her advice on how to take care of my younger brother as well as providing her emotional support as my father dealt with his alcoholism.

When I was eleven, my mother decided to go back to work as a guidance counselor. After she became more self-sufficient through working, she gave my father an ultimatum: she was going to leave unless he treated his alcoholism. I am proud to say he has not had a drink in almost 40 years. Concurrently, my mother gained confidence in herself as she worked and developed passion for her career.

What I did not realize at the time was that my mother came by her worry honestly. She was raised by my grandmother, who had grown up with three brothers during the Great Depression. For much of that time, my grandmother, a bookkeeper, was the only one in her family with a job. Like so many people of that era, she was frequently worried about money and feeding the family. She did not meet my grandfather and get married until she was 36, so she was the family breadwinner for a very long time. Then, after a miscarriage at age 39, she had my mother at 40.

As an older mother of an only child, she frequently worried about my mother's wellbeing —if she was healthy, happy, or eating enough food.

These "worrier" traits were naturally passed to my mother and then to me. So anxiety is a family legacy that I am trying to break. For me, perfectionism was a way of coping with that anxiety. If I do everything perfectly, no one will worry and everything will be OK.

CHILDHOOD TRAUMA

Childhood trauma looks different for everyone, and it impacts us all in different ways. When people think about the term trauma, they generally think of a huge life-threatening event. But that is not always the case. Psychologists have classified trauma into two different types: Big T traumas and little t traumas.

Big T traumas are what people initially think of when they hear the word trauma. These can include war, natural disasters, car/train/plane accidents, sexual assault, and similar events. Big T traumas are generally associated with the threat of serious injury, sexual violence, or death. Even if the individual isn't actually harmed, the threat creates a huge sense of fear. Big T traumas occur in response to extraordinary events that leave people with a sense of powerlessness, helplessness, or lack of control.

Little t traumas occur on a more personal level. They may seem smaller in scope, but they are still highly distressing events that exceed one's ability to cope. Examples include bullying, harassment, loss of a significant relationship, emotional abuse, financial hardship, moving, etc. These events can be extremely upsetting and can also elicit feelings of powerlessness, helplessness, or lack of control.

Another way of categorizing trauma is to look at whether it is episodic or cumulative in nature. An episodic trauma is an upsetting event that occurs one time, whereas cumulative trauma is a series of related and recurring painful situations. Often, an accumulation of little t traumas can build up, which contributes to a person feeling overwhelmed and unable to cope. At the same time, little t traumas tend to be minimized or rationalized as just being a normal part of life. When they accumulate, however, they take their toll and the individual can develop maladaptive coping mechanisms (addiction, perfectionism, enmeshment/control, people-pleasing, etc.).

When children experience an accumulation of little t traumas, they will do whatever they can to escape pain. They, too, may develop maladaptive coping mechanisms. The following examples illustrate two very different ways my patients have allowed their childhood trauma to influence their adult lives.

Susan

Susan is an attractive 50-year-old woman who'd had gastric bypass surgery ten years before she came in for therapy to address both alcohol addiction and love addiction. A human resources professional, she had been married three times. In each marriage, she got bored and had affairs with men she met at the office. She justified this behavior by telling herself that her needs were not being met at home. In therapy, she admitted that men were her "drug." They soothed her fragile self-esteem.

As treatment progressed, Susan became aware that in her childhood she was favored by her father and treated terribly by her mother. After her parents had a tumultuous divorce, her father moved away and lost contact with her. This abandonment was traumatic for Susan, and she began eating to soothe her anxiety.

When Susan was a teenager, she would get into bitter fights with her mother and say she wanted to move out and live with her father. Her mother would cruelly say, "Good luck. He doesn't want you." That truth hit Susan at a core level, and because of it, she carried a sense of shame and worthlessness into adulthood.

A great deal of Susan's adult behaviors were about challenging her core belief that she was not wanted. She desperately needed to be desired by every man to whom she found herself attracted. She would flirt with them, learn what they cared about, and figure out how to satisfy their every desire. After they began to fall for her, she would make herself invaluable to them by taking care of their every need and controlling them both sexually and emotionally. Once a man was all in, however, she felt smothered and would leave the relationship. This, of course, left a trail of devastated partners.

Until Susan began therapy, she was unaware of why all of these "imperfect and wounded men" could not get over her. In fact, all of them had stayed in her life as "friends" who were able to fluff her ego when she felt down. Unfortunately, she was exhausted from all of the acting she had to do, and from the fact she stayed constantly busy so she would not have to look at how spiritually and emotionally bankrupt she was.

Susan's continual unhealthy attempts to master her childhood trauma created chaos in her life and the lives of the men she preyed upon. Part of our work together involved building up her sober network of supportive women while developing a more accepting relationship with herself. We worked together to create more peace in her life and to end the cycle of drinking and abandonment trauma. Today, she is sober and single. She says she would like to enter into a healthy relationship and continues to heal herself so she can create a secure and loving space for that to happen.

Risa

Risa is a pretty, soft-spoken 25-year-old medical school student who came to therapy with the goal of understanding how her childhood impacted her romantic relationships. She shared that when she was growing up, her mother was frequently filled with rage and would scream at her when she made even the smallest mistake. Worse still, her mother's abuse continued into adulthood. In fact, in our first session Risa told me about how her mother had recently berated her for wearing the "wrong dress" to a family friend's wedding. Risa internalized the message that she had to be perfect, succeed in everything she did, look beautiful, and always make her family appear flawless.

After several months of therapy, Risa admitted the shameful secret that throughout her childhood her mother hit her and, on several occasions, her own anger escalated and she hit her mother back. Risa explained that she would be so upset by their violent episodes that she would begin sobbing uncontrollably. Her mother would then feel remorse and comfort Risa.

Risa told me that as a young adult, when she was upset about a romantic relationship, she would go to her mother for advice and soothing, even though her mother rarely comforted her and instead highlighted her mistakes. Risa felt she had been trained to share all of the details of her dating life with her mother so her mother could live vicariously through her experiences. She was also accustomed to looking to her mother for advice when her life felt unmanageable.

Now Risa felt her childhood patterns were holding her back as an adult looking to date and perhaps get married. Her pattern with men was to meet on dating apps where they could begin an easy banter. Once they went out on their first date, she would quickly agree to have sex because she wanted the men to like her. Because of this, her relationships would become intense quickly. For a while, this felt comforting to her. After all, Risa was familiar with and inculcated toward intense relationships —mostly because her relationship with her mother was so all-encompassing.

After a couple of dates, however, the men tended to retreat from Risa and slow the number of phone calls or texts they sent. She would experience this as a deep sense of rejection and would rage at them through texting. She would call them "users" and other derogatory terms. Even though her communication was in written form, the rage was palpable. She had learned to identify with her mother's aggression and would overreact to any per-ceived slight.

Much of our work in therapy centered around understanding the pattern she had unwillingly created. We looked at her anger and we found that underneath her rage was a deep sense of sadness that her relationship with her mother was not what she wanted it to be. She needed to grieve this relationship while also setting some boundaries with her mother. The first of these boundaries was to not share as many details about her romantic relationships. Another was not to spend as much time going home to visit her parents on the weekends. To replace those visits, she worked on developing friendships with some of the women in her medical school classes. We also began to look at what part of her family's dysfunction she brought to her dating relationships.

One of my theories about life is that we teach people how to treat us. When Risa had sex on a first date, she was showing her dates that her body was not sacred to her and they did not have to work to build a special intimate connection with her. The sex was rarely enjoyable for her because it was all focused around performance and pleasing her partner. When a man who she was dating began to slow down his communication with her, she did not let him know in a rational manner how she was feeling. Instead, she would rage at him, which resulted in her partner feeling either angry and dismissive or as small and shameful as she felt.

When Risa began to take the risk of slowing down the intensity of her connections and speaking honestly about her feelings, her relationships began to improve. Slowly but steadily, she allowed herself to be known more deeply than the initial facade she portrayed. After she learned to minimize the drama in her relationships by slowing the process, she stopped retraumatizing herself and began to become comfortable in less volatile and more nurturing relationships.

TREATING PROFESSIONAL ATHLETES AND THEIR STRUGGLES TO OVERCOME TRAUMA AND PERFECTIONISM

For the past 15 years, one of the subspecialties of my practice has been treating professional athletes who are dealing with addiction and relationship issues. This is a specialty I certainly did not seek. You see, I am not a sports fan. In fact, to both my husband's and my son's dismay, I rarely watch professional sports games. Players' names and what teams they play for seldom register with me. So in the early 2000s, when I first got a referral from the National Hockey League (NHL), I was not familiar with the very famous hockey player they were sending to me. He was just another person struggling in his marriage and feeling extremely hopeless.

Sadly, this individual had gone to several therapists before me who were at first starstruck and then completely overwhelmed by the level of anger he radiated. Because I was not impressed by his reputation as an athlete, what I saw was the scared little boy underneath the anger —a child who feared "screwing up again" and losing the wife he truly loved. I also saw the abandonment he had experienced as a child when he had to leave his family at age ten to train for his sport.

This athlete and I worked together in counseling for almost two years, and during that time he was able to become the type of husband and father he had always wanted to be, mostly through understanding his own feelings and sharing his vulnerability. Both during and after our therapy, he was vocal about how much our work together had helped him, and this led to many more referrals from NHL, Major League Soccer, and the NBA. Suddenly, this non-sports-fan was treating quite a few athletes with addictions and relationship issues.

What I have learned while treating professional athletes is that they must make a huge number of early-life sacrifices to achieve the level of excellence they seek. These early-life sacrifices sometimes lead to developmental deficits. Often, they do not grow up at home with their families (especially the hockey and soccer players) or have healthy teen dating lives or go to their proms or engage in other forms of healthy socialization. They long for their parents and normalcy, but instead they are working on their careers. Is it any wonder these athletes sometimes do not develop the social skills that accompany developmental milestones?

Many professional athletes miss out on college and on having friends who cherish them for being themselves. At the same time, the fame and financial success that accompanies the role of a professional athlete frequently causes them to question whether anyone would care about them if they were not a professional athlete.

On top of all this, living in the spotlight is difficult. Public scrutiny can be excruciating for these men, especially the ones who lack genuine self-esteem. Any mistakes they make are extremely public and come up on the news and the team's social media accounts. The public expects them to be perfect and brutalizes them when they're not. We put them on pedestals, only to knock them down when they falter. When they have an addiction or need psychiatric care, it is often difficult to keep the public at bay. Even breakups and divorces become news on Twitter and TMZ.

Additionally, professional athletes are used to pushing their minds and bodies for a "perfect" performance. Nothing less is acceptable. With statistics readily available, and coaches and agents putting pressure on them to have their ultimate peak performance in every practice and every game, there is frequently an expectation of perfection. It makes sense that they carry those perfectionist expectations to other aspects of life, including their romantic relationships.

Mike

Mike was a seasoned professional athlete referred to me by his team's medical director. Despite his large size and his over-grown beard, he had an easy smile and a sparkle in his brown eyes. We connected immediately when he shared that he had been waking up crying a lot of mornings. He had gone through a bitter divorce and was still feeling lost. His wife was a party girl rumored to have had an affair with one of his teammates. Mike was still hurting from feelings of betrayal and public humiliation after the media had a field day with this information.

During the breakup, Mike's performance suffered, and there was a great deal of speculation about whether he would be traded. However, he had worked hard to bounce back by training intensely and focusing on his health, and he was quickly back at the top of his game.

That was when he met another woman, Laurie. Laurie was a seductively dressed fan who knew how to shower Mike with attention. She was "up for anything" and would accompany Mike when he traveled to other cities. He found her exciting and spontaneous until he realized how severe her cocaine addiction was. Their lovemaking was passionate but their fights were epic. After six months of dating, he sent her away to a west coast rehab. When she returned, she had given up hard drugs but still drank alcohol and smoked pot frequently.

Mike knew Laurie was dangerous for him. They would have frequent "blow out fights" that kept him up until all hours of the night, but then they would have great "makeup sex." He tried to date other women but always seemed to end up back at her place late at night, stuck in a dysfunctional pattern.

Finally, in one of our sessions, he shyly asked if I could do him a favor. He asked if I could meet Laurie and let him know what I thought. He explained that he trusted me and did not trust people very often. His family was really far away and rarely met any of the women he dated. They had hated his ex-wife but he had married her anyway. He told me that he was now starting to doubt his own judgment because he had been so badly burned. He was paying his ex-wife alimony even though she was the one who cheated, and he still felt completely betrayed.

Before agreeing to his request, we talked about what my opinion would mean to him. He told me he liked me because I was honest with him and not afraid to tell him what I thought. In some ways, I reminded him of his mother. I asked him what he meant by that, and he explained that his mother was not afraid to speak her mind and was a very strong woman. He further shared that she had been brave in her marriage to his father, who was a violent alcoholic. She had done everything she could to curb his father's drinking while still managing to drive all over the country, taking Mike to his games.

The following week, he brought Laurie to the session. She had jet black hair, a lot of eye makeup, and wore skintight jeans and a skimpy camisole. She sat very close to Mike, stroking his arm while we spoke. Within a few minutes, it became apparent that she had no hobbies or interests other than being a professional athlete's girlfriend. She worked for her father's cleaning supply company, which enabled her drug use. If she woke up tired or hungover, she did not need to show up for work and was still paid enough to buy whatever she wanted. She could also travel with Mike on a moment's notice. When she drank too much at a local bar, she could call Mike and he would drop whatever he was doing in order to "rescue her."

I found myself in what felt like a precarious position because I believed Laurie was a disastrous choice as a girlfriend for Mike, and I was sure he was going to ask my opinion the following week. Additionally, because of his celebrity status, I knew he was surrounded by a lot of people who were not honest with him and whom we jokingly called his "yes men." During the next session he looked at me and read my face before I even responded to his question, "What do you think?" We talked about how Laurie had not found herself yet and was not emotionally ready to be in a relationship with him. We also began to discuss his attraction to dangerous women whom he could save. Then we began to discuss the damaged soul of his father, whom he could not rescue. Mike's perfect fantasy in a relationship was that he would find a "damaged" woman and then make himself invaluable by saving her.

Over the next several years, I met three more of Mike's girl-friends. As he became healthier, the women he dated began to mirror that. He began to look at his enmeshment issues with his family of origin along with his own alcohol and drug use. In time, he realized that his dark side craved seductive women who could bring an intensity to the relationship that was similar to the adrenaline rush he had when he played an exciting game. He also got in touch with some of the chaos he had experienced watching his parents' abusive relationship while he was growing up. As he began to grieve for the boy who felt overwhelmed and scared because of his father's alcoholism, he let go of his need to try to fix wounded women.

The last woman he brought in to meet me was a beautiful kin-dergarten teacher. She radiated a wholesome energy as she spoke about her love of children. She was a runner who took care of her-self by jogging each day, and she had a strong support network of female friends. She and Mike spoke about getting engaged before he was transferred to another team, which, at that moment in his career, seemed likely. Best of all, Mike's smile seemed genuine as he talked about life with his soon-to-be fiancée and thanked me for helping him find his way. He was now aware of the pull his past has on him, and he had developed the skills he needed to avoid reenacting the trauma from his childhood.

EXERCISE 1

Write about what your patterns in relationships are. How do those patterns relate to your childhood? Are you trying to avoid getting hurt again? Are you trying to control someone else's behaviors?

EXERCISE 2

Be the family historian. What were your parents' struggles? What about your grandparents' issues? If you do not know, interview a family member. Ask them about adversity in your grandparents' lives? Write the themes down and make connections to your own life. What has been your traumatic legacy? What patterns do you need to break? Explore these ideas in your journal over the course of several days.

3

WHY STAY TOGETHER?

KEEPING IT REAL

As a psychologist specializing in addictions and relationships, I need to make a full disclosure: I met my husband in a bar. It was 27 years ago when we first locked eyes at Rock Lobster, a popular outdoor bar on Delaware Avenue in Philadelphia. He was a handsome young lawyer with a warm smile. We had an easy banter, and although we had never met before, we quickly realized we had several friends in common.

On our first date, he disclosed to me how tough his last year had been. He shared that he had recently failed the Bar Exam and was subsequently fired from his job. He told me how ashamed he was, and he described a painful experience of going to the office holiday party right after he'd received his test results and no one would talk to him the entire night. The following day he was fired. Since then, he'd retaken the Bar Exam, passed with flying colors, and was hired at a firm that felt like a better fit for him.

Hearing his story helped me to quickly develop compassion and empathy for him. His disclosure displayed honesty and a sense of vulnerability that attracted me. It also encouraged me to share some of my own moments of both failure and success, and we forged a deeper bond.

I told him that before meeting him, I had been in a relationship with a charismatic man who frequently lied or "stretched the truth" to appear as he wanted to appear.

Honesty, authenticity, and vulnerability were essential qualities I wanted in my life and from my partner. Twenty-seven years later, we still strive to keep those qualities at the center of our relationship. Some days it is easier than others. In a world where many people edit their versions of the truth, I strongly advocate for "keeping it real." For my recovering patients, I encourage sharing about their addiction history early on in their dating experiences. If someone is turned off, then he or she is not the right person.

Life gives us many forks in the road: moments when we must decide whether to show the glossy "perfect" view of ourselves or the unflinchingly honest and real version. I unequivocally advocate for honesty. Perfection is both overrated and boring. Honesty, vulnerability, and risks lead to more peace within ourselves and greater depths in our relationships.

SHAME

One core reason that people are not honest with each other is that they carry shame. John Bradshaw describes the difference between shame and guilt very well. He explains that with guilt you feel like you made a mistake and with shame you feel like you are a mistake. Guilt happens when you feel bad about your actions, and shame happens when you feel bad about who you are as a person.

Shame is much more pervasive than guilt, and it often takes root during childhood. When a child grows up and experiences disappointments and traumas, the child often internalizes the experience and believes that the negative experiences happened because he or she *deserves* bad things and, even worse, that he or she *is* bad.

Shame and perfectionism are related. If you do not feel good enough about who you are as a person, you may try to hide your authentic self from others. What this looks like in a relationship is when a person lies about mistakes that were made and tries to put on a false front of being perfect. Or if a partner does not allow himself or herself to be anything less than perfect because he or she does not want to be uncovered as a fraud. The only way to overcome shame and have a relationship that lasts is through taking risks and being honest.

Jason

Not long ago, I treated Jason. As a child, he had been neglected by his parents and was sent away when he was 11 to a boarding school, where he was sexually abused by a teacher. As an adult, because Jason was used to feeling shame and carrying that secret, he continued to feel shame and carry secrets in his marriage, never telling his wife about his feelings of inadequacy, his struggles in his high-powered job in commercial real estate, his cocaine use, or the fact that on two occasions he had visited prostitutes. His wife, Stella, had no idea about the double life her husband was leading and actually said to him on more than one occasion, "We are so lucky that we have the perfect marriage." It did appear perfect on the outside. They had a beautiful modern home and three well-behaved children —two young sons and a daughter.

In his therapy with me, Jason learned he had to accept and address some of his character defects, such as dishonesty and people-pleasing. In her own therapy, Stella realized that she thought her marriage was perfect because Jason never disagreed with her. He tried to people-please constantly and always told her what she wanted to hear. He also managed to be the perfect chef and caretaker of the children. He was fearful of exposing the truth and being rejected. Because of that, she actually had little idea about who Jason really was.

Jason's moment of reckoning came when he lost his job. His boss uncovered the web of lies he was spinning at the office, as well as the fact that he was using cocaine. Suddenly, Jason's "perfect persona" came crumbling down. In my office, he came clean to Stella about how out-of-control his life had become. He shared how he had learned to lie at five years old in order to hide his struggles at school from his parents. He further explained that he was already an accomplished liar when he was away at boarding school and was "perfect prey" for his young teacher, who realized quickly that Jason could (and would) keep secrets.

When Jason first exposed his secrets and lies, Stella was furious. The fact that her "perfect" husband wasn't so perfect was difficult for her to accept. He had presented himself as being extremely successful at work and assured her that he had made some great financial investments. This turned out to be a "house of cards." They also had purchased a home that was more than they could afford and realized they would have to downsize.

Much of my work with Jason was about confronting the realities of his life instead of seeing life the way he and Stella "wanted it to be." This was not easy. Stella had a quick temper and did not handle disappointment well. Jason had to work hard at being honest and saying no to Stella instead of just trying to please her by telling her what she wanted to hear.

Although both Jason and Stella had to learn to tolerate anger and disappointment, over time their relationship improved. They also began to know each other on a much deeper level. Best of all, they addressed their challenges as a team, including finding a more modest home and Jason finding a more suitable job where he could be himself instead of wearing his mask of the "successful persona."

As Jason and Stella became more honest and real with each other, they also became more transparent and accepting as parents and addressed their younger son's learning disability by switching him to a private school for children with learning differences that was better equipped to help him thrive. Through the hard work of honesty and authenticity, this couple managed to stay together and make the changes that supported the growth of their family.

CHARACTER DEFECTS AND HOW THEY IMPACT RELATIONSHIPS

The concept of character defects has been well described by Alcoholics Anonymous. In fact, part of doing 12-step recovery work is identifying coping skills that no longer work for you. These could be traits that helped you when you were a younger, more defenseless person. For example, not telling the truth to a physically abusive parent may have saved you from getting beaten as a child. However, being dishonest as an adult in a loving marriage creates chaos and destroys the trust you desire. Dishonesty, which started as a coping mechanism, has become, over time, a character defect.

Character defects can also be considered assets gone astray. For example, you might feel a genuine desire to help someone, which can turn into a desire to fix that person and sacrifice your own self in the process. Identifying the behaviors and character traits that no longer work for you is essential so that you do not unconsciously bring those issues to your relationship.

Sometimes, despite your best intentions, your character defects become apparent to your partner and your partner's character defects become obvious to you. The challenge in these situations is to remain committed to your relationship by working on your own issues without attempting to control your partner's issues. In the addiction recovery community, we call that "staying on your side of the street." If each person is able to be honest and accountable about how their less-than-ideal behaviors impact the relationship, then the couple can work through the tough moments and grow together.

WHY STAY IN YOUR RELATIONSHIP?

Why should you bother with the challenging, often painful process of working on your relationship? It may be easier to just cut and run, starting fresh with a clean slate and a new partner. If you do that, you do not have to engage in individual and couples therapy, where you have to rehash, relive, and re-feel pain, disappointments, and failed expectations.

In the, admittedly rather silly, movie *Shall We Dance*, stars Richard Gere and Susan Sarandon share one of the best quotes about why to stay married that I have ever heard. In the film, Richard Gere's character has a secret he's keeping from his wife: he is taking dance classes. Susan Sarandon's character knows that her husband is hiding something from her, but she's unsure what. Because of this, she suspects that he's having an affair. She hires a private investigator to follow her husband, and the private investigator asks her, "If you feel like you can't trust him, why are you staying?"

She answers by saying, "In a marriage, you are promising to care about everything. The good things, the bad things, the terrible things, the mundane things. All of it, all of the time, every day. You are saying that your life will not go unnoticed because I will notice it. Your life will not go un-witnessed because I will be your witness."

Although we are all on our own life paths, it is incredibly valuable to have a witness, someone who truly knows you and can be present with you through the journey. It is my belief that this is why most of us choose to stay in our marriages, even when the going gets tough.

TWO QUESTIONS I ASK AT THE BEGINNING OF A COUPLES THERAPY SESSION

I often start a couples therapy session by asking, "What have you done to help your relationship this week?" This is a very powerful question because it changes the couple's mindset. Instead of pathologizing the problems in their marriage, it turns the focus to what they have done well. It also sets up the image of them working as a team to help rescue their relationship.

After I ask this question, there is often a pause as each member of the couple reflects back upon their successes the previous week. They each have the opportunity to share a behavior that makes them feel proud. This experience also helps them reframe small gains as essential contributions to the health of a relationship.

After listening to the couple share the positive behaviors they have contributed, and providing supportive feedback and reassurance, I ask them my second question, "What have you done to hurt your relationship this week?" This question normalizes the fact that we all do things that harm our relationships. It implies that despite our best intentions, we all engage in behaviors that are not ideal.

For individuals who are coping with illusions of perfection, this question is freeing. It can be a springboard to address deeper patterns in their relationship, or it can simply provide an opportunity to examine a situation where they "blew it."

As we look at what each partner did that did not go well, we are able to practice working through shameful feelings in order to help each person listen to the other. There is also an opportunity for accountability, apologizing, and forgiveness.

My hope in implementing these questions is that the couples I treat will begin to reframe their small positive interactions as successes, and will look at their struggles as not being the end of the world. My longer-term hope is that after several sessions in couples therapy, they will be able to check in with each other on a weekly basis and ask themselves these questions without a therapist present.

Carol and Jay

Carol and Jay began couples counseling during the COVID-19 pandemic. Our first appointment was a Zoom therapy session, and even over a computer screen I could see that this was a couple in trouble. They had a seven-month-old baby and took turns holding her during our entire session. They were obviously overwhelmed trying to manage full-time jobs along with attending to their baby's needs. Additionally, they were trying to comply with all of the precautions that were necessary to keep their family free from COVID.

The reason Carol and Jay sought counseling was that they did not agree on some important relationship issues. As a new mother, Carol was reluctant to bring a babysitter into their home. She was desperately afraid that their baby would catch the coronavirus. She had strong convictions that both she and Jay should work from home and take turns caring for their baby themselves, without bringing in any other caretaker.

As a new father, Jay was concerned about financially providing for his family. He owned a gym, which he believed was at risk during the pandemic. He felt it was essential for him to go there in person to keep the business functioning and to show that it was safe for his patrons to be there, as long as they followed the proper precautions. Jay held the strong conviction that it was necessary for the two of them to hire a babysitter to help with childcare.

In addition to conflicts about childcare and working from home, Carol and Jay were struggling to emotionally separate from their families of origin. Each of them was constantly defending their parents' beliefs. Both partners were rigidly stuck in their own positions and wanted me to say who I believed was right. There was a lack of empathy for each other's concerns, and very little compassion for the pain their partner was experiencing.

When I first asked Carol and Jay the questions about helping and hurting their relationship during the past week, they both looked at me blankly. Coming up with what they did that hurt their relationship the previous week was easy for them: each had been quick to point out their partner's flaws. Identifying the positive aspects was more of a challenge because I was asking them to change their perspectives. They hesitated at first, but then became aware of the little things they were each doing to try to help their relationship. "Jay saw I was tired and gave the baby a bath." "Carol bought my sister a birthday present."

We spent our first several sessions working on communication skills, mostly how to listen to each other's concerns. During the fourth session, Carol mentioned casually that the only affection she ever received during this time was when she cuddled with their baby. After I told her how sad that made me, her eyes filled with tears. She explained that during the pandemic she had not hugged or even touched her parents or her sister.

I took her disclosure as an opening and asked both Jay and Carol about physical affection with each other. Jay admitted he had not hugged or kissed Carol in months. When I asked why, he reluctantly admitted he was mad at her.

I showed empathy for Jay's situation and admitted that I know what it is like to be angry with someone. At that point, I made a personal disclosure and shared about a time when my husband and I were experiencing some ongoing conflict. I told them that at that time, although the issues my husband I were struggling with were not resolved, we decided to take a radical step forward by giving each other a passionate kiss every morning before we separated for the day.

I do not often share personal disclosures like this with my patients, but I believed Carol and Jay could benefit from hearing about my struggle, and that sharing it would help them know I understood the power of holding onto resentments and that I had empathy for their situation. Also, I believe it is important to model that sometimes you have to work at showing affection, even if you are not completely over your pain. Happily, Carol and Jay agreed to do just that by giving each other a romantic kiss each morning.

In our next therapy session, before I could even ask what they did that helped their relationship the previous week, they both began talking, eagerly telling me that the act of kissing each other every day had become a new ritual they both enjoyed. Better yet, they both found that the physical affection of kissing helped to ease relationship tension. Instead of Jay feeling guilty that he was leaving their home, he felt supported. Instead of Carol feeling abandoned and judged because of her cautious beliefs, she felt comforted. Best of all, instead of waiting for forgiveness before showing affection, the act of showing affection led to a connection that fostered forgiveness.

In 12-step recovery there is a slogan: bring the body and the mind will follow. For Carol and Jay, the act of providing affection through romantic kisses was a way to bring their bodies forward so their minds and hearts could follow. For this couple, the act of kissing released oxytocin, the feel-good hormone. It also reminded them that they do have a special and loving connection.

The simple act of asking questions during therapy about what the couple did to help and hurt their relationship uncovered a major issue for Carol and Jay —a lack of physical connection. Recognizing and addressing this issue changed the couple's focus from working against each other to working together to focus on the positive aspects of their relationship. It made them a team committed to reviving their relationship. Although they still have work to do as they navigate the stress of transitioning into their roles as parents during a pandemic, they are now committed to making their relationship their highest priority.

SHOULD I STAY OR SHOULD I GO?

Although this book advocates for staying together and working through relationship struggles whenever possible, sometimes it is not in our best interest to stay. The questions below can help you determine what the best course of action may be for you. Unfortunately, there is no definitive formula for deciding if your relationship has enough positive attributes to warrant the difficult process of working on it. However, through the process of honestly answering the questions below you will likely gain some clarity. Feel free to go over your answers with your therapist, 12-step sponsor, or a close and supportive friend.

1. **Is there physical violence in your relationship?** You should not stay in a physically abusive relationship. The psychotherapist Mira Kirshenbaum clarifies this issue, writing, "Abuse that happens more than once means you must leave the relationship. Otherwise, it will happen again and again and it will get worse, and your self-esteem will fall and your sense of being trapped will grow." I believe that if there is even one episode of physical violence that causes the possibility of injury or death, there is nothing to discuss. You need to leave immediately for the sake of your physical safety. Kirshenbaum further expands on this topic by saying that the "only exception is when the abusive partner is currently, actively, and motivatedly participating in a program designed to treat abusive partners and stays in the program for at least a year," and that while this is happening the abuse has stopped. Although domestic violence is beyond the scope of this book, it is worth saying that if physical violence occurs, there are resources, including women's shelters and other spousal abuse resource centers, that can help you create a plan to leave your relationship quickly and safely.

2. **Were things ever really good in your relationship?** This is an important question because it leads to other questions. Were you ever in love? Were you ever genuinely happy together? Kirshenbaum states it simply, "You can often fix what was broken, but you can rarely fix what never worked in the first place." In other words, a relationship that was never very good is not likely to become good in the future. An analogy for this concept is buying a house. When you go to buy a house, even if the house looks messy and the wallpaper is ugly when you first see it, if it is solid and sturdy underneath all of the dirt and clutter, you can clean it up and have a beautiful home. On the other hand, there are

houses that may look great on the outside but there is structural damage on the inside due to a poorly laid foundation. They may have water damage or a major termite infestation. You do not want to invest in a home that is truly rotten in its foundation. If you can't remember a single point in your relationship when you were truly happy together, then it does not have a good foundation and it may be time to leave.

3. **Do you and your partner have a couple of pleasurable activities you both enjoy?** A relationship where the partners share at least a few common interests is often worth saving. Some examples include: having friends over for dinner, cuddling in bed, doing crossword puzzles together over a couple of cups of coffee, watching movies together, going to the dog park, playing racquetball, or cooking gourmet meals together. This does not mean you and your partner have to share every interest, but you should have at least a few recreational pursuits that you enjoy doing together.

4. **Do you actually like each other?** Step back from any temporary anger that is occurring in the moment and ask yourself if you truly like your partner and if you believe that your partner likes you. Do you enjoy spending time together, or do you dread that moment when your partner walks through the door? Although no couple likes each other every moment of every day, it is important that you are mostly comfortable and happy to be with your partner the same way that you genuinely enjoy being with a friend. Also, does your partner make you feel like you are liked and cared about?

5. **Do you trust each other?** It is difficult to recover when you are in a relationship that has experienced a breach of trust. However, many relationships do survive even the pain and betrayal of infidelity. But it is almost impossible to recover if you believe

that everything out of your partner's mouth is a lie. When you are in a committed relationship, you often are in a position to trust the other person with your home, your finances, your kids, and your feelings. If you don't believe that your partner is capable of honesty, it is time to reconsider your investment.

6. **Do you still want to be touched by your partner?** What about sex? Is it still good together? It is important for couples to engage in physical touch, including kissing, hugging, holding hands, and rubbing each other's shoulders. Sometimes in anger there is a mutual shut down of sexual behaviors. Wanting to touch and be touched by your partner is a sign that there is still a physical and emotional attraction. Desiring physical touch is an important indicator that there is still some chemistry there, and it is worth working to end the shutdown. Enjoying physical intimacy is important in finding your way back to each other.

7. **Do you share core values and beliefs?** Although no two people have the same exact set of values and beliefs, there needs to be some common ground. It is important to share some of the same views regarding religion, politics, finances, and raising kids. Without those commonalities, you are coming from two different playing fields and you may have a difficult time compromising or understanding each other.

8. **Do you and your partner usually find a way to resolve differences?** Conflicts will inevitably occur in your relationship as no two people see things in the exact same way. When this happens, are you able to work through the disagreements in a respectful manner or is one person silently seething with resentments? Does one member "hit below the belt," saying incredibly cruel insults to the other? Are your arguments growth opportunities

where each person learns about and develops empathy for the other one, or is there an invisible scoreboard?

9. **Do you both generally feel respected?** If one member of the couple is constantly silencing the other one and not listening to his/her opinions, the other one will feel disrespected and may shut down and refrain from speaking. This can lead to distance or a power struggle. One member may want to "take charge" at all times and be dismissive or curt with the other. This is not helpful for the relationship. In a healthy relationship, each person should feel listened to and respected.

10. **Do you have kids?** I am not implying that having kids together is the only reason to stay in a relationship, but it is a reason to think long and hard before leaving. After all, your decision to leave impacts not only you but your children. My friend, the esteemed therapist and author Robert Weiss, eloquently says, "Breaking up a family is a significantly more profound decision than splitting up a couple because the lives and futures of several people, some of whom may be too young to fend for themselves, are at stake."

11. **Are you both fully invested in saving your relationship?** Are you both willing to do whatever it takes to save your relationship, including going to a good couples therapist, writing in a journal, or going to a couples workshop? It is difficult to resurrect your relationship if only one of you is invested in trying to save it.

12. **Have you cut and run before?** Is it your pattern to disappear when a relationship becomes difficult? Is your perfectionism leading you to leave as soon as you face hurt and disappointment? It may be worth it to stick around and work on yourself before you flee for greener pastures.

EXERCISE 1:
Helpful and Hurtful Behaviors

As a couple, find a quiet place to sit down together at the end of the week. Separately, write down several things you did that helped your relationship during the past week. Keep these statements short—one or two sentences at most.

Next, separately write down a few things you did that hurt your relationship over the past week. These statements should also be short—one or two sentences at most.

When both of you have completed your lists, take five to ten minutes to share your statements, both good and bad, with your partner listening and (hopefully) expressing empathy.

Taking stock of your behaviors in this way helps you to become more aware of how your behaviors impact someone else. And when you and your partner share your lists and listen to each other without being defensive or judgmental, you will feel like you are working as a team to try to improve your relationship.

EXERCISE 2:
Regrets, Requests, and Appreciations

The purpose of this exercise is to spend some time alone thinking about what you regret doing, as well as what you want from your partner and what you value about him/her. After some time reflecting, list your thoughts and then share what you came up with, preferably in the safety of the therapy room. Your partner should do this exercise as well.

"I Regret..." List the things you have done that you believe were harmful to either yourself or your partner, and that you do not intend to repeat.	"I Request..." List the things you want your partner to do for an improved relationship.	"I Appreciate..." List the traits and behaviors of your partner that you like and admire.

EXERCISE 3:
RELATIONSHIP QUESTIONS

The purpose of this exercise is for each partner to spend some time reflecting about the relationship and what it means to him/her. After you and your partner each journal your answers to the questions listed below, you should each share what you came up with. This can be a powerful experience when thoughts are communicated within the therapy room. Even couples who have been together for decades tend to learn valuable pieces of information about each other.

1. How do you see your relationship today? Describe how you would like your relationship to be in the near future, where you would experience more intimacy, connection and fulfillment. Develop action steps to take you from where you are today to where you want to be.

2. What do I believe my partner expects from me? What do I expect from my partner?

3. What behaviors have created distance and hurt in the relationship? List which behaviors you are willing to change.

4. What messages from your family of origin have you repeated in your relationship?

5. What are your strengths? What are your partner's strengths?

6. How are you and your partner alike? How are you different?

7. What are your hidden dreams?

8. Complete the following sentences:
   a. In our relationship, I am happiest when...
   b. In our relationship, I am saddest when...
   c. In our relationship, I am angriest when...
   d. The best thing about our relationship is...
   e. I am most afraid when...

f. I feel most loved when...

g. I feel appreciated when you...

h. My greatest fear for our relationship is...

i. The feelings I have the most difficulty sharing with you are...

j. I feel most grateful about...

4

LEARNING FROM PAIN

TRANSCENDING THE CRISIS

OK, so there was an explosion in your relationship and you are wondering how you're going to make it through the day, not to mention the rest of your life. Whether it was an extra-marital affair, the uncovering of an addiction, a financial betrayal, or an act of dishonesty, you feel lost and you are wondering what happens next. Before I give you any advice or suggestions, just breathe. Breathe in. Breathe out. It is all going to be OK. First off, you do not have to make any decisions right now.

What you do need to do is take care of yourself. Be loving, gentle, and kind with yourself and take some responsibilities off your plate. That may mean asking a friend or family member to drive your carpool, it may mean ordering in dinner, it may mean not weeding the flowerbeds this week. Just let go of any superfluous responsibilities and treat yourself like you are your own best friend. Get a massage. Spend time outdoors. Watch a sunset.

Do not attempt to handle your relationship crisis alone. This means asking for help and relying on your support team. It is OK for you to feel (and look) like a hot mess. It is OK to share about what you're going through with someone you trust. If you do not feel safe sharing your situation with local friends due to the fact that they are your partner's friends, too, call your long-distance friends. Summon your angels! Call, text, or email any and all of the safe people in your life who love you unconditionally. Ask them to come see you ASAP. The ones who truly love you will. You can also call a trusted therapist or member of the clergy for support. The point here is that you do not need to handle the weight of the world alone.

Begin a journal. Your voice is important. There is meaning in your pain. Write it down. You'll find that you have more answers than you know.

You can also set boundaries. Chapter 7 will share a thorough discussion about the topic of boundaries. For now, I will simply say that boundaries are guidelines, rules, or limits a person identifies to create safety. Some examples of boundaries you can set around your relationship are: your significant other does not need to stay in the house. He or she can stay in a hotel, with family, or with a friend. Or your partner can stay in the home but sleep in another bedroom until you feel safe. If your partner is addicted (whether the addiction is admitted to or not), you can insist that he or she needs to go to and complete a stay in rehab to remain in the relationship. You can take off your wedding ring if you no longer want to wear it. You can leave the house if you want to, staying with a friend or family member. You can figure out some of these boundaries with a therapist, and they can change as you grow.

My most important takeaway for you is this: although this situation sucks and the pain is overwhelming, it does not have to break you! You are more than this pain and you will endure. You have lived a life before this betrayal and you will live a life after it. To paraphrase Gloria Gaynor, you will survive.

FROM SURVIVING TO THRIVING

In the words of the famous author Elizabeth Gilbert, "The women whom I love and admire for their strength and grace did not get that way because shit worked out. They got that way because shit went wrong and they handled it in a thousand different ways on a thousand different days, but they handled it. These women are my superheroes."

How do we start viewing ourselves as superheroes and not simply victims who are stuck in our misery? Well, first off, we realize that no one gets out of life unscathed. We all experience pain. It is how we deal with pain that defines us. Although we are hurting, a small part of us understands there may be some value to the pain. Israeli philosopher Martin Buber explains, "All suffering prepares the soul for vision." Pain has a purpose of allowing us to know that situations must change.

Alexandria

Several years ago, I worked with a patient named Alexandria. She was an incredible woman —a nurse who was raising three daughters while working full-time. Alexandria was married to her best friend, whom she had met in college. They had a strong marriage and were raising their girls in a home filled with a great deal of love.

Alexandria had grown up in family with a strong mother, and found it easy to parent. Her father was a recovering alcoholic who left most of the "heavy lifting" of parenting to her mother. After being married 20 years, Alexandria realized that she had been unconsciously repeating her mother's model by trying to handle everything herself. She was great at making life look easy by juggling working full-time and taking care of the majority of responsibilities with the children, as well as entertaining and cooking gourmet meals every night. She even dressed immaculately and always had a smile on her face.

Below the surface, however, Alexandria was exhausted. She was resentful of her husband, who was frequently working or spending time with his friends playing golf. When she discovered that he'd had an affair, she was devastated. The betrayal hit her at her core but also allowed her to get off the "hamster wheel" that was her life.

When Alexandria came to therapy, she learned that she did not have to be perfect, which had been her role since childhood. Growing up, her job was to make the family look good. She'd taken that same role in her adult life by taking care of her patients, friends, and family members.

During her period of healing, Alexandria decided to reduce her hours at work and to take the summer off from cooking. During that time, her husband learned how to barbecue and the family also began to order in for dinner. At the same time, Alexandria learned how to be vulnerable with her friends instead of only showing them her supportive caretaking role.

While Alexandria was lessening the responsibilities that she was taking on and seeking greater understanding of herself, her husband was working on himself too. He looked at the loneliness and sense of inadequacy he was feeling that derived from his own chaotic upbringing. He began to look at how in childhood he "checked out" when he was screamed at by his unstable mother. The affair was his way of "checking out" once again after feeling as though he was not receiving the approval from his wife and children that he craved. In my office, both Alexandria and her husband began to examine how they could be present for each other as well as change the roles in their relationship. Her husband began the work of reengaging as an active father and committed husband.

Although Alexandria was devastated and had to grieve the loss of the "perfect" relationship she thought she had, the crisis in her marriage presented her with an opportunity to challenge the perfectionistic way she was living. She finally stopped sending out her perfect Christmas cards where even the dog was looking at the camera.

FINDING THE MEANING IN OUR HEARTACHES

When my daughter was one year old, my husband and I were enjoying Chinese take-out on the floor at a friend's house. It was a cold winter day. We were eating out of Chinese food cartons on paper plates and enjoying time with our friends while my daughter crawled around us. As I watched her, she saw the bright fire burning in the fireplace and started crawling towards it. At that moment, I felt like time froze and that I then started moving in slow motion. I realized she was going to try to touch the vibrant orange logs and I was not going to be able to get to her in time to stop it. My stomach dropped as she put her hand out to touch the fire before I could grab her. We quickly called the pediatrician, who advised us to put her hand in freezing water as quickly as we could, which we did in our best attempt to stop the damage from a third-degree burn, that fortunately healed completely after several weeks.

What this incident taught me is that sometimes, even when we see pain coming, we are not able to save our children (or anyone else, including ourselves) from experiencing it. I will always remember that moment when time stopped and I realized I was powerless to protect my daughter from the pain she would have to endure. Other lessons learned centered on the importance of baby-proofing our house, not using the fireplace for several years, and being very cognizant of when we went out to houses that were not babyproofed.

Fast forward to 17 years later and this same daughter was a senior in high school going through a difficult time with her girlfriends. Basically, she was feeling excluded and hurt by her group of friends. There was no way I could protect her from that either. I loved her deeply but was unable to stop the pain. What I did not realize until then was that there is a value in staying present and being a loving witness. When she decided to write about her experiences and created a TED Talk describing girl exclusion as a way to help other young women who were suffering, I realized that her pain had created a depth of understanding and empathy she would not have had otherwise, and she was able to use that to help others. Who knows what the value of our pain may have for our future?

If you are struggling in your marriage or in your relationship with your children, please know that you are not alone. There is meaning to be found in your pain. The challenge is figuring out what the life lesson is. Years ago, I worked with a young woman who struggled with an eating disorder. After working on herself and her relationship with food, she realized that her ultimate superpower was her ability to educate others about eating disorders. She became one of the country's most successful fundraisers for the National Eating Disorders Association. This young woman discovered her life's purpose in her ability to help others heal.

AFGOS

When I find myself going through a period of trauma or loss, I often say, "This will make me a better therapist. Through my own pain, I will develop more compassion, empathy, and understanding of others." Years ago, I had a supervisor who coined the term AFGO.

What it stands for is: Another Friggin' Growth Opportunity. My point is that it is not just a meaningless cliché to say that what does not crush us makes us stronger.

MY AFGO

In the spring of 2014, I had a lot on my plate. My private practice had expanded its scope and suddenly I was in charge of supervising four therapists while also treating a full-time caseload of patients. Additionally, I was the parent of three children of varying ages and needs, and I found myself running in a million different directions to get them to their different schools and activities. Somehow, in the midst of all of this chaos, I had agreed to chair a fundraising event for charity that culminated in an Outdoor Cocktail Party/Tennis Exhibit in the middle of the week. The event had gone off seamlessly, and I had even given an eloquent speech.

The following morning, I woke up feeling thoroughly exhausted. I had taken the morning off from work, so I dropped off my son at preschool and started driving to the gym. Even though I was tired, I told myself that after I worked out I would feel better. Suddenly, out of nowhere, a huge truck crashed into my SUV. I don't remember what came next, but apparently it was a pretty bad accident. Airbag going off bad. Car totaled bad.

Even though the truck was on my side of the street, I blamed myself. If I weren't so tired, my reflexes would have been quicker. Why was I driving if I was so exhausted? Couldn't I have just skipped the gym and gone home to sleep? What if I had gotten someone else to drive my son to school and just stayed in bed? What if he were in the car? These and other negative thoughts and questions ruminated in my head. I blamed myself for the accident and wanted to hide.

As an extroverted person, I usually connect with friends when I want to feel better. I tend to talk things through and gain comfort from my support system. Not this time. After the accident, I went through a period of post-traumatic stress where I just wanted to isolate. I did not want to get back in a car. I didn't even want to get out of bed. I felt sadness and shame as I blamed myself. It took me over a week to recalibrate. As this occurred, I realized I needed to slow down and work less. I needed to say "no" to extra commitments. I even needed to socialize less and spend more time alone. With those realizations, I decided to spend the summer working less and leaving time for myself to heal.

This was a rough lesson to learn. I literally had to be hit by a truck to realize I needed to slow down and take better care of myself. Over time, I learned to listen to my body and ask for help when I needed it. I didn't have to be Superwoman. I could just be a human being. While this AFGO taught me to have more empathy for myself, it also showed me how to have more empathy for others who have experienced trauma.

Paul and Janine

Several years ago, Paul, a pediatrician, called me during the biggest crisis of his life. He had just discovered that his wife of thirteen years, Janine, had an affair with a guitar player in a local band. The couple had five children together, ranging in ages from four to twelve. Paul was blindsided because he thought they had the perfect marriage.

During the several months before Paul called me, he had noticed that Janine had been going out on more "girls' nights" with her friends from the gym and was often coming home drunk. He had excused the behavior, believing that she deserved to blow off some steam after spending so much of her day as a stay-at-home mom to their five children. Their youngest had special needs and was especially draining.

After learning about the betrayal, Paul was devastated and was not sure if he should end the marriage or try to save it. His primary fear was that if they separated, his children would unravel, just like he did when his own father had an affair and left their family.

When I met Janine, she shared that she had just been so lost. Both of her parents had recently died after long illnesses and she felt like she was suffocating during all of that sadness. She was overwhelmed with the demands of raising young children while her husband escaped to the comfort of his office and the patients and their families who adored him.

Moreover, Janine was a warm, outgoing woman who missed being her fun younger self. When she met some animated new friends at the gym, the thought of going out to bars and dancing along with the local bands was intoxicating. She began to resent Paul for being quiet, studious, and boring. Her new friends encouraged her to soak up the attention of the lead guitarist in the local band. His compliments and flirtation made her feel exciting and special, which was so different from how she felt during her everyday life.

When the guitarist's wife discovered the infidelity, she called Paul to reveal the affair, and she publicly humiliated Janine (and Paul and her own husband, the guitarist) by exposing the cheating all over social media—not to mention the parents' page for the Catholic school that both couples' children attended. She also threatened to physically harm Janine if she came near her husband again.

Paul and Janine were shell-shocked by the drama and trauma the affair had caused. Because of that, part of our work together was focused on slowing down the anxiety and blame that they were placing on each other in their attempts to create a sense of safety in the relationship. Each of them needed to stop talking over each other and simply listen to what the other was saying.

For example, Janine needed to feel heard before she could begin to look at how alcohol had fueled her behaviors. She eventually agreed to go to Alcoholics Anonymous, even though she was not sure if she had an alcohol addiction. Once she began attending the meetings, she formed some healthier female friendships that were supportive of her desire to work on her marriage as well as change some of her behaviors. Additionally, she began to look at how her resentments with Paul had accumulated and how truly lonely she was. She had not grieved the loss of her parents or the struggles involved with having a special needs child.

Meanwhile, Paul had a difficult time forgiving Janine because his ego was badly injured. It was hard for him to look at his part in their struggles and how he was not emotionally present while she was grieving the loss of her parents. And, instead of talking about the struggles of raising a special needs child, he had always acted like it was no big deal and then retreated to his office, leaving Janine feeling guilty and ashamed for feeling overwhelmed. Paul had to examine the fact that maybe their marriage was not perfect and at times his wife felt lonely.

Additionally, Paul and Janine had to work through their personality differences. Paul was introverted, needing few friends, while Janine was extroverted with a strong need for socialization and intimacy. Neither of them was feeling particularly appreciated by the other. Ultimately, Paul and Janine shared the same values of raising children well with strong character and love, and were both invested in making their marriage work. Once the illusion of a perfect relationship was shattered, they began to participate in the hard work of building an honest, more genuine connection.

One of the most important things Paul and Janine learned from their pain was that they really wanted their marriage to work. They realized they needed to prioritize their time together by having date nights or just going on walks together. They also craved time away from cell phones and children's schedules where they could openly talk.

I suggested, among other things, that the two of them begin walking the dog together around the neighborhood in the mornings. This ritual of coming together with a shared purpose of connecting started their days off in a much more intimate way. Also, time away from cell phones, whether in a restaurant or in their own backyard, was crucial for them to feel like they were each other's top priority.

Janine's affair also taught her the value of being more selective about who she spent time with. She realized that hanging out with girlfriends who had encouraged her to "party" and live hedonistically was not in line with her core values. She also became aware that after her parents died, she had been isolated from her siblings as they had all sunk into their own grief. Connections with her sister and brothers were important to her and she recommitted to spending time with her extended family. Janine also began individual therapy and started to process her own grief as well as her struggles in mothering. Janine also realized she missed working outside of the home and began working as a florist in a local flower store on a part-time basis. She realized that her need to feel valued had contributed to her having an affair. Most importantly, she began to speak up in her marriage by asking Paul for help when she felt overwhelmed.

Paul learned that the affair had triggered him to feel abandoned. Gaining awareness of these feelings allowed him to recognize that this was how he felt as a child when his parents divorced. As a young boy, he had coped with the pain by escaping into books, and he'd become studious and hardworking. This behavior had helped him gain some attention and accolades from his preoccupied parents.

During stressful times in Paul and Janine's marriage, he had escaped by spending more time at the office. Unfortunately, this behavior was not helping their situation. Eventually, Paul began to look at his workaholism as well as his inability to express his feelings. The affair allowed him to focus less on his career and more on his emotions. He realized that he deserved time to grieve, too.

As Paul slowed down, he realized that he had neglected his own self-care in order to be a successful physician and a present father. He had not shared the pain of the infidelity with a single friend and had let go of his hobbies and exercising time. Gradually, Paul began to take better care of himself and joined a weekly bicycling group. With my encouragement, he also shared his vulnerability with a college friend by telling him about his struggles in the marriage.

A blessing that resulted from the affair was that both Paul and Janine prioritized their marriage as being a foundation for their family. They realized that they still loved each other and needed to better nurture their relationship with each other as well as their relationships with themselves.

A TOUCH OF GREY

One of the most iconic rock bands of all time, The Grateful Dead, has lyrics that say, "Every silver lining's got a touch of grey." What I believe these lyrics mean is that no situation is perfect. Even in the most idyllic life experience there is some pain. It challenges the illusion that there is some perfect happy ending. The song closes in a powerful way as the band sings out their chorus, despite the pain, "We will get by. We will survive."

Both my patients and I have learned through our "grey periods" that our pain causes us to take stock of our lives and even grow. To expand on The Grateful Dead's Lyrics, we will not only survive, we may even thrive and be better than before. We may increase our ability to have empathy, compassion, and kindness for ourselves and others.

EXERCISE 1

Think about a supportive person you loved who is no longer living. It could be a parent, grandparent, teacher, or mentor. Now imagine yourself telling that person about the pain you are currently experiencing in your relationship. Then imagine what this person would say in response. Write this supportive person a letter explaining what you are feeling. Then write a letter in response from the supportive person to you. Think about the advice, love, and direction this person would give you if he or she were still alive. Include this in the letter, allowing this person's voice to guide you in your writing.

EXERCISE 2

There is meaning in your pain. What are the lessons you have learned through this experience? List them. Once we notice all that we have learned, our suffering does not have to feel purposeless.

EXERCISE 3

Make a relationship timeline of all of your romantic relationships and describe what you have learned from each of the relationships. Are there any themes? In completing this exercise, you will realize that there is something to be learned from all of your past relationships, even the painful ones.

5

WHEN YOUR LIFE
HAS MORE DRAMA THAN
A REALITY TV SHOW

REALITY TV SHOWS

I have never been a fan of reality television. Truth is, I have enough drama going on in my own life between my patients' situations and the drama in my frenetic household where my husband and I are raising three children. However, I realize I am in the minority and that reality TV has quickly become a large part of popular culture. In fact, this acceptable form of voyeurism gives millions of people a release from their own unexciting lives and careers and allows them to be spectators of a more glamorous (or, sometimes, a far less glamorous) lifestyle.

Reality shows provide us the opportunity to live vicariously through other people's struggles and triumphs. We get the false sense that we know those people on the screen. In this way, reality shows can fill an emotional void. For some viewers, the shows can provide wish fulfillment as we pretend we are enjoying a more luxurious side of life. The characters may even start to feel like they are our friends and we are actual participants in their lives. According to Psychology Today, the less connected we feel to people in our lives, the more likely we are to seek the drama and pseudo-intimacy of reality TV.

Conversely, because these characters' lives often look like train wrecks, we have the opportunity to feel superior. The numerous fights and confrontations the characters experience allow us to feel better about our own struggles. We see their awkward situations and vicariously live through their heartache all the while feeling superior. Our lives don't seem to be quite so bad.

THE KARPMAN DRAMA TRIANGLE

As a psychologist specializing in healing from addictions and relationship betrayal, I am frequently confronted with very difficult situations in relationships. One thing I have learned is that the pain involved in an unhealthy relationship can be enormous, yet people will stay stuck in their discomfort without taking action for many years.

Why?

When confronted with this overwhelmingly difficult question, I like to answer in the simplest possible terms. Recently, I have been using Stephen Karpman's Drama Triangle, developed in 1968, to explain the nature of dysfunctional relationships and why people stay in them.

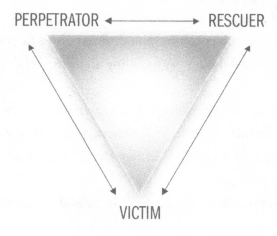

Karpman explained his triangle as a social model of human inter-action, where there is a map of destructive interactions that can occur between people in conflict.

At the bottom of the triangle is the victim role. This is the per-son in a relationship who feels oppressed, helpless, hopeless, powerless, ashamed, and unable to function effectively. This is the person who says, "Poor me." The victim struggles with solving problems and with finding pleasure in life. This is a person who chooses not to be accountable and therefore does not gain insight into the situation. The victim often feels depressed and ashamed.

The victim position is so painful that after a while it tends to become intolerable. Because this position in the triangle is so excruciating, the victim will eventually move to one of the other roles. For example, the victim may take on the rescuer role, saying, "Let me help you." This is the role of an enabler. The benefit of the rescuer role is that when the rescuer focuses all of his or her energy on someone else, he or she can ignore his or her own anxiety and issues.

The negative effects of the rescuer role are that it can keep the vic-tim (the person who is being "rescued") dependent. It gives the victim permission to fail. Additionally, when a rescuer feels a lack of self-worth, that person will keep trying to prove his or her value by "doing more," even when what that person is doing is no longer welcomed by or help-ful to the victim. Examples of this include compulsive caretaking, doing all of the work around the house, handling all of the childcare responsi-bilities, etc.

As occurs with the victim role, the rescuer role can eventually feel intolerable. When this happens, the rescuer typically feels resentful, like a martyr. At that point, the rescuer may switch roles, perhaps entering into the perpetrator role.

The perpetrator is the victimizer. This individual is the villain, the offender who acts out his or her anger and rage. The perpetrator may say, "It is all your fault." A perpetrator is often controlling, blaming, critical, oppressive, rigid, and superior. He or she acts entitled and shows anger through bad behavior, possibly through screaming or being physically, emotionally, or sexually abusive.

The perpetrator's victimization of the other person in the relationship may be overt, such as being physically abusive. It can also be covert, such as having an affair. The perpetrator's behavior is a way of indulging in entitlement or displaying rage. It may involve compulsive shopping, gambling, or drinking. After acting out with those behaviors or in some other way, the perpetrator feels terrible and may switch roles, perhaps to being a victim or trying to make up for bad behavior by moving to the rescuer role.

As you can see, the Karpman triangle is a triangle of dysfunction. There is very little health on this triangle, yet partners often stay stuck in it for years on end, bouncing from one role to another. I have often seen individuals and couples lose decades to this dysfunctional dance.

Interestingly, the only way out of the drama triangle is through vulnerability. A person must risk the pain and shame of looking at and owning his or her behaviors. Therapy is a process that can help individuals look at the roles they play in the drama triangle while sharing their feelings of pain and the fears that lurk beneath the surface. Through honest sharing of emotions, individuals and couples can find more straightforward ways of relating to each other that can ease them out of the drama triangle.

Joey and Melissa

Joey and Melissa were a couple in their late thirties who had been married for several years when they first arrived in my office. Melissa worked in retail and had a cool urban vibe to her. She dressed in baggy jeans, trendy t-shirts and often wore a wool cap to complete her look. Joey had brightly colored tattoo sleeves down his arms. He dressed in all black with motorcycle boots and often wore leather. He would frequently drive his Harley Davidson to my office. They came in for treatment because Melissa was extremely frustrated by Joey's heroin use. He had gone through a detox program where he had stopped using all narcotics but had relapsed several times since he had gotten out of treatment, at least partly related to his work as a nurse at an emergency room where he had access to pain pills.

After assessing the situation, I decided that Joey could benefit from attending a 30-day rehab program and, despite some initial protests, he agreed to go. Once he left the facility, he participated in an aftercare program which included attending 12-step meetings, individual counseling, and continuing couples therapy with me. Unfortunately, Joey was reluctant to follow the treatment team's recommendations and chose not to go to Alcoholics Anonymous or Narcotics Anonymous meetings. He thought he would feel uncomfortable sitting in a room with a bunch of strangers and believed he could handle sobriety on his own.

Shortly after returning, he relapsed again. At this point, Melissa was beside herself. Her love for Joey was apparent, but she contemplated leaving the marriage. She cried in our sessions, saying that her dream of being a mother was never going to happen. She and Joey had wasted many years in this cycle and her child-bearing years were quickly passing. The difficulty was that when Joey was sober, he was an incredible husband and partner to Melissa. Their love was apparent and he was thoughtful, kind, and supportive; however, when he used drugs, he was unreliable and deceitful. He would not come home for days on end and would be argumentative and angry when he returned.

In an emotional session, Melissa decided to give the relationship one more try. I supported her decision but gave Joey the ultimatum that in order for me to continue as their couple's therapist, I would need him to follow all of my treatment recommendations, which would include going back to rehab for another 30 days, then moving to a half-way house where he would need to continue to work on his sobriety and attend daily meetings. In 12-step programs, they recommend doing a "90 in 90." This means attending 90 meetings in 90 days. So I recommended that as well. On top of all of these requirements, I recommended that he leave his job in the emergency room because it was highly stressful and provided ready access to drugs.

The good news is that Joey had finally hit bottom. He was willing to surrender and to follow all of my recommendations. He felt desperate and did not want to lose the love of his life.

While Joey was away in treatment, Melissa came to my office for support. She began to look at her own piece in their dynamic and started attending Al-Anon meetings where she looked at her dependency, enmeshment, and enabling issues. She looked at the caretaking she did and began to step away from the dysfunctional aspects of her role as Joey's caregiver.

In treatment, Joey learned that "half measures avail us nothing." He realized that the half-hearted way that he was following his treatment team's recommendations kept leading him to relapse. He also began to look at some of the cognitive distortions that kept him stuck in this cycle. This time, after completing his inpatient stay, he willingly moved into a half-way house where he agreed to live with ten other recovering men for three months. He would leave the house to attend 12-step meetings on a daily basis, and to continue weekly couple's therapy sessions with Melissa at my office. He also took a leave of absence from his job to fully immerse himself in a life of recovery.

In couples therapy, we looked at both Joey and Melissa's roles on the Karpman Triangle. Joey's triangle would start in the Rescuer Role. He would work selflessly as a nurse in the emergency room. His schedule often varied and he was always available for whatever hours the team needed. Joey would work tirelessly attending to his patients' care until he became resentful. He would feel taken advantage of and then begin to switch roles by taking on the Victim Role. "All I do is work," "No one appreciates how hard I am working." He would feel depressed and not valued. These feelings allowed him to move to the Perpetrator Role of entitlement, where he could justify swiping medication from his patients. "I deserve this pain pill." After victimizing patients as well as himself, he was in a position to victimize Melissa by lying to her. These behaviors created a great deal of shame and unworthiness, which brought Joey back to the victim role, where he felt depressed and anxious, and avoided spending time with Melissa.

Melissa's position on the Karpman Triangle often started in the Victim Role, where she felt lonely, sad, and anxious due to Joey's disappearances while he was doing drugs. She would then move to the Rescuer Role, where she would frequently check their bank account to see if he took money out of the ATM. She would call his work to see what time he left in order to account for his missing time. She would handle all of their finances, clean the house, cook all of their meals, and schedule Joey's doctors' appointments to make things easier for him. She would then begin to feel like a martyr, resentful about how much work she was doing. When Joey would finally return home, Melissa would switch to the Perpetrator Role by raging at Joey. She would feel entitled to verbally abuse Joey, but then would feel badly about the way she spoke to him and would start to feel like a victim again.

After dissecting their patterns on the Karpman Triangle, both Melissa and Joey realized how much they needed to improve their communication skills with each other. In therapy, they learned how to address their feelings instead of acting out their pain in dramatic ways. They even began to attend a weekly Couples Meeting in AA in order to make healthy couple friendships. Eventually, the love they had developed became even stronger.

Additionally, Joey realized that he needed to quit his job. After he did that, he was able to find a less stressful position as a nurse in an outpatient pediatric practice. Although his new job is not as challenging and at times might even be a little boring, he has regular daytime hours and is able to attend his 12-step meetings on a consistent basis. Additionally, now that Joey has achieved over two years in recovery, he and Melissa realize that they will have their need for excitement fulfilled because they are expecting twins!

EXERCISE 1

What role(s) do you play in the Karpman triangle?

What role(s) did you play in your childhood, and how are you maintaining that now in your relationship?

If possible, can you share your discoveries with your partner?

EXERCISE 2

What can you do to break out of the Karpman triangle? Create a list of any practical steps you can take to free yourself from this triangle of dysfunction.

6

WHAT ABOUT FORGIVENESS?

FORGIVENESS AND GRATITUDE

*"To forgive is to set a prisoner free
and discover that the prisoner was you."*
— Lewis B. Smedes

*"All negativity derives from fear. When someone is angry,
they are afraid. When someone is rude, they are afraid.
When someone is manipulative, they are afraid.
When someone is cruel, they are afraid.
There is no fear that love does not dissolve.
There is no negativity that forgiveness does not transform."*
— Marianne Williamson

In 2002, the director of the Stanford University Forgiveness Project, Dr. Fred Luskin, described forgiveness as a feeling of peace that emerges as you take your hurt less personally and take responsibility for how you feel. Both Luskin and Dr. John Gottman, founder of the Gottman Institute, describe a distress-maintaining scenario called a grievance story. They explain that when we have trouble forgiving someone, it is because we put on a selective filter and select only those elements of the experience that support our own perception of events. This creates a sense of righteous indignation as we recall the most negative aspects of the person and his or her most hurtful actions. We then view the most virtuous and innocent aspects of ourselves, filtering out any personal shortcomings. Maintaining this mindset supports our own grievance stories, where we are victims and therefore allowed to harbor and nurture resentments. Luskin urges us to change our grievance story to a forgiveness story, where we become the hero instead of the victim.

Forgiveness does not change the past, but it does change the present. It does not take away your pain. It does, however, mean that even though you are wounded you are choosing to hurt and suffer less. Hurting is a normal part of life and is a reality when you are in a relationship with someone else. There is no relationship that is pain free.

More importantly, just because you choose to forgive someone does not mean you are necessarily going to stay in the relationship. You have choices. You can forgive and rejoin the relationship or you can forgive and never speak to that person again. The act of forgiveness is for you and no one else.

TURN ON THE BEAUTY, FORGIVENESS, AND GRATITUDE CHANNELS

When we stay stuck in our grievance story, we spend all of our time focused on grudges, anger, and wounds. We lose sight of the good aspects of our lives. Luskin describes the act of picturing yourself changing the trauma channel on a television. I have used this analogy with many patients who are caught up in their grievance story. I ask them to picture their television sets and all of the many channels that are available to watch. Instead of staying on the trauma channel, I ask them to envision themselves switching to the beauty channel or the gratitude channel. If they turn on the beauty channel, they could embrace nature shows or appreciate incredible music. They could also notice the taste of a delicious meal, the sight of a field filled with wildflowers, or the tantalizing aromas around them.

I then ask my patients to picture themselves switching the station to the gratitude channel. I ask them to imagine themselves walking into a supermarket filled with an abundance of delicious food. I tell them to picture themselves saying thank you for having so many options available. Then I take it a step further by asking them to imagine themselves walking into a hospital or a nursing home and saying thank you for the fact that they are healthy when so many people are not.

After they have a moment to contemplate their good fortune, I ask them to remember any kind act done to them by their parents or other family members. Additionally, I ask them to give a silent prayer of thanks for small acts of kindness, such as when they walk into a store and a salesclerk offers help. I also speak of the value of mentally thanking each of the drivers who are following the rules of the road. There are so many little things that we take for granted when we are not watching the gratitude channel.

Lastly, I ask my patients to turn on the forgiveness channel. When you are looking at the world through the lens of forgiveness, you notice people who have forgiven others. I urge my clients to ask people they know who have forgiven others to tell them their stories. I also ask them to remember a time in the past when they themselves have forgiven others. I remind them that they can do this again. I suggest that they read books about people who have forgiven others and to search for forgiveness stories in their own families. I suggest that they practice forgiving even the smallest offenses that are done against them, whether it is a waitress who brought them the wrong order or an acquaintance who messed up the pronunciation of their name. The act of forgiveness is like exercising a muscle. It gets stronger with each bit of practice.

HOW TO FORGIVE

Dr. Robert Enright, the founder of the International Forgiveness Institute, explains, "When you forgive someone who has deeply hurt you, you let go of resentment and the urge to seek revenge, no matter how deserving of these things the wrongdoer may be. You give the gift of acceptance, generosity and love. Though the wrongdoer does not deserve these gifts you don't let it stand in your way. You give not out of pity, not out of grim obligation. Rather you give because you have chosen to have a merciful heart. A heart with the power to free yourself so you can live a better life."

When we hold on to our hurts, we become emotionally and cognitively stunted. As a result, many of our relationships tend to suffer. In my practice, I have seen forgiveness become the best remedy for healing that pain. Often, we consciously know this, but we don't have the tools to let go of our wounds and begin the forgiveness process. My patients and I often struggle with how to forgive, especially when we have been deeply hurt.

In my practice, Dr. Enright's theories have been instrumental in guiding my patients through the forgiveness process, and in my own life, have helped me significantly. In his book, *8 Keys to Forgiveness,* Enright defined eight components of the forgiveness process. I have adapted these six which have been the most helpful for my patients.

1. **Recognize what forgiveness is and why it is important.** Enright describes forgiveness as, "goodness and extending mercy to those who've harmed us even if they don't deserve it." Although this definition is simple, it challenges us to change our focus to our

capacity for generosity and kindness instead of staying in the victim mentality. It is crucial to recognize that forgiveness benefits both the person you are choosing to forgive, and also the forgiver. Some of the psychological benefits of forgiveness include decreasing depression, anxiety, and unhealthy anger, as well as lessening the symptoms of post-traumatic stress disorder.

2. **Address your inner pain.** It is important to figure out where your psychological wounds are coming from. Are you angry at your partner or are you really angry at your parent for abandoning you? What type of emotional pain are you experiencing? Is it anger, depression, anxiety, lack of trust, or low self-esteem? Find a safe, supportive place to figure out what you are feeling. Talk through your emotions with a trusted friend or therapist who can help with this process.

3. **Develop empathy.** Research shows that when someone successfully imagines forgiving another person, there is an increased activity of the neural circuitry responsible for empathy. The best way to strengthen your ability to show empathy is through examining some of the details in the life of the person who has harmed you in order to gain a better understanding of the trauma that person has carried. One way to do this is through creating a narrative comprised of the facts you know about this person, as well as using your imagination to add to the story. Although your frustrations may color your perceptions, thinking about people's struggles from this new perspective may provide you with compassion for their psychological suffering. This helps you to humanize the other person and realize the pain you both share.

4. **Find meaning in what you have endured.** Without seeing meaning in the pain, you can lose your sense of life's purpose

which can lead to hopelessness and despair. In order to discover meaning, ask yourself, "How has the suffering changed me in a positive way?" This may be difficult to do at first, because it is easy to stay stuck in a negative mindset. Reframing your pain into positive life lessons is crucial to healing. I encourage you to avoid minimizing your pain by using self-talk like, "I'll just get over it," or, "Everything happens for a reason." Glossing over the adversity in your journey is a missed opportunity. Instead, take time to figure out the gifts and resiliency that the pain has given you.

5. **Forgive Yourself.** This is easier said than done and it's a challenge that we are all constantly working on. Grasping the understanding that we, as human beings, are imperfect and are going to make mistakes is one of the core themes of this book and my practice. Even if you've acted outside of your own morals or ideals, it's crucial to forgive yourself so that you don't engage in self-punishing behaviors such as avoiding friends and family members, overeating, or excessive drinking and drug use. Along with developing compassion for others, it's important to soften your heart toward yourself and to take the time to develop the self-compassion you deserve. Only after you forgive yourself, can you authentically offer a sincere apology to someone else.

6. **Develop a Compassionate and Forgiving Heart.** One of the benefits of overcoming suffering, is that we gain a profound understanding of what it means to be humble, courageous, and kind. When we heal from pain, we gain the ability to see we are not the only people hurting in the world. This deep level of awareness that suffering is universal allows us to create a culture of forgiveness in our homes, schools, and workplaces. Additionally, we become more aware of the hatred, violence, and victim-

izing that goes on in our communities, and can create the space within ourselves to do our part to protect our world.

AN EXAMPLE OF FORGIVENESS IN POPULAR CULTURE

In popular culture, one of the most heartwarming examples of forgiveness I have seen in a long time occurred on the Apple TV show *Ted Lasso*. The main premise is that a British Premier League soccer team owner, Rebecca Welton, is trying to get back at her philandering ex-husband by hiring an incompetent team coach, Ted Lasso, to lead her ex-husband's beloved team.

By hiring a small-time American football coach with no soccer experience, Rebecca hopes to relegate the team to the minor leagues. As Rebecca explains it, "My ex-husband only loved one thing in his entire life: this club. And Ted Lasso is going to help me burn it to the ground."

Throughout the show's first season, Rebecca tries to sabotage Ted at every opportunity, setting him up to fail with the media, players, and fans alike. However, Ted's unflinching optimism and kindness make him hard to dislike. He has an incredible way of always seeing the best in other people and managing to do right by them.

At a pivotal moment of the season, Rebecca admits to Ted that she has been sabotaging him and never had faith in him as a coach in the first place. While she is making this confession to Ted, you can see the pain in his eyes. At this moment, he is at a low point in his life: his marriage has crumbled, he is not seeing his son, and the team has been relegated to the lower league. Now he finds out that the woman who has been lovely to his face has been incredibly cruel behind his back. So Ted looks directly at Rebecca and says simply, "I forgive you. Divorce is hard."

More than just saying the words, it is apparent that Ted truly does not hold on to any resentments or anger about the betrayal. He goes right back to work with Rebecca without quitting and focuses on the future not the past.

We all have experienced betrayals and disappointments in our lives. To watch an example of someone who so gracefully and with humility practices forgiveness inspires us all to want to be better people and to forgive others more frequently. I have shared this example with patients in several different predicaments, whether it was a work situation where my patient was feeling disrespected or a romantic situation where there was rejection. I have used Ted Lasso's life lessons on forgiveness and optimistic reframing as an aspirational goal.

THE QUILT ANALOGY

Several years ago, I counseled a couple who both looked at me with tears in their eyes and asked, "How can we ever move past the hurts and betrayals in our marriage?" Their pain was so raw that I knew no educational fact about forgiveness would get through to them. I gazed directly into their eyes and shared the analogy that helps me. When I think about a long-term marriage, a relationship that spans decades, I visualize a big, beautiful quilt. A quilt can be incredibly gorgeous, even if not all of the squares on it are perfectly sewn. The color on one square could have a darkness to it. That does not necessarily mean that the quilt is ruined. In fact, it adds character, life, and imperfect beauty.

Ellie and Marc

Ellie and Marc had been married for twenty years. They had weathered many storms together, including the death of Marc's father and the trials and tribulations of raising three kids. Their marriage had always been a beacon of strength for them and had provided solace through the ups and downs of life.

Recently, however, they had each been feeling disconnected and lonely. Their children's needs were increasing and Ellie was exhausted as she put more time into their school work and emotional development along with meeting the demands of her own job. Her oldest daughter was 16 and trying to navigate dating, "mean girls," and learning to drive. Her younger children were struggling with the rigorous academic curriculum in their respective schools. At this time, Ellie was relying on her girlfriends to meet her emotional needs and feeling resentful as she managed the children's stressors alone.

At the same time, Marc, still reeling from the death of his father and was feeling detached from his children as well as his wife. He started going to happy hours after his workday and began a flirtation with a significantly younger woman who worked at a marketing firm his business had hired. She was not married or focusing on the struggles of raising children and could put all of her energy into complimenting Marc. Before long, he began an affair for the first time in his twenty-year marriage.

Ellie noticed Marc's absence as well as his irritability and tried to talk to him about it. She even suggested counseling. Marc, however, was dismissive of her concerns and said that every marriage had its ups and downs and he was just going through a down period. Ellie believed him but her resentment grew. While teaching her daughter how to drive, her daughter told her that she was shocked that her father wasn't helping. "I haven't even had a conversation with him in weeks," she said. This wasn't like her father, who had always been actively involved in her upbringing.

The following week Ellie received an email from the roommate of the woman Marc was having an affair with. The two women were in a fight and she decided to try and hurt her room-mate by revealing the affair to Ellie. Ellie was devastated. For the whole length of their marriage, with all its ups and downs, she had been absolutely certain that they were in it together. There was never a threat of infidelity or any other flirtation that would compromise the integrity of their relationship. Initially, Marc tried to deny the allegations, but then admitted it and begged Ellie to stay in the relationship and begin counseling. He ended the extramarital relationship immediately and said that he would do whatever was needed to rebuild their relationship.

When Marc and Ellie first came into my office, I saw how much pain they were both experiencing. Neither of them had an appetite and neither was sleeping at night. "We're thinking of ending our marriage," they said. I felt sad for them because despite this affair and their stressful recent year, they shared with me many beautiful memories from a successful and fruitful long-term marriage. After I shared with them my quilt analogy, I could see that it resonated.

I asked them to envision a quilt representing their marriage, and yes, there was a dark patch in the middle of it. "Your job," I said, "is to add as many light and beautiful squares around that dark square as you possibly can." I assured them that it wouldn't take away the dark square but there could still be beauty and splendor in the huge and hugely imperfect quilt they were sew-ing together. "Now visualize hanging up the sacred quilt in your living room where you can appreciate it every single day."

The act of picturing this quilt was important because it didn't ignore that the hurt and pain that occurred and would always be a part of their journey together. It simply provided a visualiza-tion that life could still be beautiful despite the darkness. The act of forgiveness does not remove pain; it just chooses to build love and beauty around it.

GRATITUDE

Gratitude is an expression of appreciation for what you have and a conscious effort to count your blessings. University of California professor Robert Emmons broke down the definition of gratitude into two components. The first, he explained, is an affirmation of goodness. "We affirm that there are good things in the world, gifts and benefits we've received." The second component is recognizing that the sources of this goodness are outside of ourselves. "We acknowledge that other people—or even high powers, if you're of a spiritual mindset—gave us many gifts, big and small, to help us achieve the goodness in our lives."

What I like about Emmons' definition is that there is a relationship-strengthening component to it. According to his definition, gratitude encourages us to see how we've been supported and affirmed by other people. It is the polar opposite of narcissism, cynicism, and isolation. Instead of not trusting others, gratitude encourages us to count our blessings, especially the support we get from other people in our life. The following example illustrates how even during an awful year of losses, it is possible to display gratitude.

Jerry

Jerry, thirty years into recovery from alcoholism, had experienced a terrible year. He was let go from his 20-year job as the CEO of a furniture company after the company was in danger of going bankrupt. There were false allegations that he had stolen from the company due to a bitter employee's anger after being terminated. The whole environment at this family-run business had become toxic, and there were several employees who weren't doing their jobs and were looking for someone to blame. Jerry became the scapegoat. Additionally, Jerry's mother-in-law had recently died from a COVID-related illness and his wife was distraught.

Upon the recommendation of his sponsor, whom I had counseled years earlier and had offered support during his recovery process, Jerry began therapy with me. At our first meeting, he was extremely anxious and believed that his own recovery was in jeopardy. One of the best things about working with Jerry was that he followed directions. When his sponsor suggested he begin therapy, he did not hesitate to call.

Jerry had a difficult time forgiving himself for the mistakes he made at work and at home. He regretted hiring the employee who had anger issues. He also blamed himself for not leaving the company sooner. He felt like he had given his "heart and soul" to this company and had sacrificed time he wanted to spend with his wife and daughters. Additionally, his wife was angry with him for not being more present when her mother suddenly got sick. Plus, Jerry couldn't believe that after giving so much of himself to his work-life, his reputation was now in jeopardy. He felt like he couldn't win in the workplace or at home.

Jerry worked hard in therapy reprioritizing what was important to him and became much more communicative with his wife and daughters. He followed therapeutic advice and joined a men's therapy group in addition to attending daily AA meetings to reconnect with his support network. He also attended couples therapy sessions with his wife so they could work through their issues. He began meditating again. He visualized forgiving himself.

Gradually, Jerry realized that being let go from his job was a blessing. He left a toxic environment and had more time to focus on his recovery program. He realized that his life goal was to write a book on recovery instead of working as a CEO. Each day he would feel gratitude as he worked on this writing project that was so meaningful to him. He would connect with people he cared about on a daily basis and actually began to feel the love around him.

We reduced our sessions as Jerry felt stronger, but then he received another life challenge. He sent me a text with a picture of the first floor of his house that had been destroyed in an electrical fire. I assumed he would be devastated and offered to fit him in as soon as possible for an emergency therapy session. He replied to me that he did not need it and would see me the following week as scheduled. He told me that he was just feeling so grateful. None of his family members were in the house during the fire and he had so many people in his support network who were there for him. He told me that he was the luckiest man in America.

In my opinion, life is not about the blows that we receive; life is how we handle those blows. Instead of feeling resentful and angry when his house burned, Jerry felt grateful. He realized that insurance would cover the financial aspect of the damage and that the most important thing was that his family members were safe. And he was able to appreciate the love and support his family and friends were showing him.

Jerry also expressed gratitude for my check-in emails and said that he was grateful to be working a strong recovery program at a point in his life when he really needed it. His resiliency was incredible, and he thanked me again for the care and concern that I always offered him.

In our final session, Jerry shared a story with me. While he was standing outside of his house watching it burn, the local firemen drove up in their firetruck to help. A moment after they parked their truck a large burly bearded fireman jumped out of the truck and gave him a big bear hug. "I'm just so sorry for your loss," he said. When Jerry looked at him, he realized that this was a man he had known for years from their AA meetings.

His family members were puzzled as they observed this loving act of humanity from a local fireman. Jerry was so moved by the support and concern that his fellow AA member and, in fact, all of the firemen had shown to him and his family that he plans on throwing them a barbecue next summer after his house is rebuilt. He plans on inviting his supportive friends, too. To me, this is the ultimate act of gratitude. Instead of focusing on what was lost in the fire, he is celebrating the love, support, and friendships that remain indestructible.

TURN YOUR STORY AROUND

I have never been an early morning person. My family knows that about me and tries not to put too many demands on me before 8 a.m. Unfortunately, this year my son's school bus picks him up at 7 a.m. In order to give him a good start to his day, I've been getting out of bed early to make breakfast and help him get organized before he leaves the house.

To be honest, the thought of getting out of a warm bed on a freezing cold winter morning fills me with dread. However, this morning as we were eating our breakfast together, I looked out the window and saw the most gorgeous sunrise. As I gazed up at the sky filled with shades of lavender and pink, I realized how beautiful it was. I even took a picture to document the sacredness of the moment.

After my son left for school, I had an hour while the house was quiet to drink my coffee and write. Here is what I wrote: At this moment in time, I am feeling gratitude for the beauty of the sunrise, which I would have missed if I'd slept through it. I am also grateful for the quiet time to sit at the computer. Today, instead of looking negatively at the hardships in my life, I view them as opportunities to receive gifts.

EXERCISE 1

Start a practice of listing three things per day that you are grateful for. This simple act changes where you focus your attention.

EXERCISE 2

List three acts per day that you forgive. It could be small acts or big acts. For example: when someone cuts you off while driving, if a waitress brings you the wrong order, or if a friend does not call you back. The act of practicing forgiveness for small offenses is helpful in creating your capacity for larger acts of forgiveness.

EXERCISE 3:
A FORGIVENESS PRACTICE THAT CAN HELP YOU DEVELOP AND GROW YOUR ABILITY TO FORGIVE

This practice was inspired by the writing of Stefanie and Elisha Goldstein in "11 Ways to Forgive" in the April 2017 issue of *Mindful Magazine* and should be done once a day in order to strengthen your forgiveness muscle.

Think of someone who has caused you pain and whom you're holding a grudge against. Visualize a moment when you felt the most hurt by this person and then acknowledge the pain you still carry. Focus your energy on your unwillingness to forgive. Now observe which emotion is present. Do you feel anger, resentment, or sadness? What do you physically feel? Where is the pain in your body? Do you feel tenseness or heaviness? Now focus on your thoughts. Are they spiteful or filled with despair? Allow yourself to feel the burden associated with the pain that still lives inside you. Now ask yourself:

Who is suffering?

Have I carried this burden long enough?

Am I willing to forgive?

If the answer to the last two questions is still "no," that is OK. Some hurts take longer to heal than others.

Here is a meditation that can help with healing. Silently repeat to yourself, "I breathe in and acknowledge the pain. I breathe out and release this burden from my heart and mind."

The simple act of practicing this meditation can help us release some of the pain and anxiety associated with holding on to negative feelings.

EXERCISE 4

Hang your own memento symbolizing the love that still remains in your relationship. In the Jewish religion, couples sign a Ketubah, which is a marriage contract that represents the commitment and responsibilities they share. This is often hung on the wall. There are many ways to create your own representation of your commitment to one another. You could hang a picture, a quilt, or a poem. A visual representation honors your ongoing commitment despite the imperfections in your relationship.

7

STAYING PRESENT
AND SEEING OTHERS

DOES YOUR FACE LIGHT UP?

One of the most important life lessons I've learned came from the writer Toni Morrison in an old interview I watched. Morrison described how when a child enters the room and looks at her parents, what she is searching for is to see if their faces are lighting up. Are their eyes sparkling? Do the grown-ups in the room care if she is there?

So often, parents are preoccupied with their cell phones, spending too much time checking their texts and emails, worrying about the next event they have to attend or their next deadline. When they do pause to notice their child, it is usually to focus on the child's imperfections. The parents may tuck in their son's shirt or fix their daughter's hair. They may believe that this is caring for their child by trying to fix him or her and making sure the child looks presentable. However, the message the child receives is that he or she is not good enough the way he or she is.

I heard the interview with Toni Morrison when my children were babies, and I have always tried my best to allow my eyes to sparkle whenever they walk into a room. There are times, however, when I still must consciously stop myself from "fixing them," focusing instead on just allowing my face to light up as I take in their incredible presences.

Over the years, I have expanded this concept, applying it to not only what children crave but what everybody craves. Whether it is the cashier at the grocery store, our colleagues at work, or our partner greeting us at the end of a long day, we all long to know that we are seen, appreciated, and that we matter.

Psychotherapist and blog writer Katherine Schafler expanded upon this topic by stating there are four questions that we are unconsciously asking each other all the time. The four questions are:

1. Do you see me?
2. Do you care that I am here?
3. Am I enough for you, or do you need me to be better in some way?
4. Can I tell that I am special to you by the way that you look at me?

Although these questions are often unconscious, when the answer is yes, we feel appreciated and loved. Whether your children, your friends, your colleagues, your partner, or anyone in your community truly feels valued by you, you have answered these four questions in an affirmative way.

One of the reasons that dogs are so universally loved is because they answer these four questions consistently with a giant YES! Dogs are creatures that live in the present moment, and they are happy whenever we are in that moment with them. Dogs do not hold grudges that their walks were too short the previous day. They are not living in the future worrying about what they will eat tomorrow. Dogs live in the here and now. Humans often fail in this arena. And what that looks like for us is disconnection.

In my practice, I hear people expressing dissatisfaction and feeling isolated. They say:

- "He didn't even look up from his computer when I walked into the room."
- "She's standing right in front of me but it's like she's looking past me."
- "He was so obsessed watching the ball game that he didn't even notice I was there."
- "While we were out to dinner, she spent the whole night checking her phone."

How do we change this?

We take an extra second to look at the other person. We allow our eyes to sparkle as we smile. We truly connect. Connection is not based on the amount of time we spend with someone but the quality of our presence. Being present does not require meditation, deep breaths, or any mantra. It is simply a decision. "OK, I am going to be present now. I will smile with my eyes and listen to what the other person is saying. I will do my best to communicate that I am happy the other person is here." This does not need to be communicated in words; it can be shown non-verbally on your face, in your touch, with your eyes, and with the quality of your presence.

FINDING YOUR ZEN FOR MEDITATION FLUNKIES

There seems to be an unwritten rule that all holistic therapists are supposed to recommend that to help reduce distress and anxiety, their patients should begin a meditation practice. This recommendation has become so popular that it feels "on trend," like eating kale or doing yoga.

The goals of meditation are aimed at managing the constant barrage of thoughts and stimuli that clouds our minds and encourages people to "be in the present," to unplug and focus inward. Many therapists suggest meditation apps or that their patients find private meditation classes.

While meditation is a great tool for many people, it requires commitment and doesn't always work for everyone.

Several years ago, I thought I would give meditation a try, so I Googled "meditation classes nearby." I did not find many options that were close to where I lived and at times that were convenient for a working mother. Finally, I did find one class that I could attend, and I enjoyed it, but found it difficult to incorporate it into my schedule on top of my regular cardio workouts and other life commitments. Then, that meditation studio moved out of my area.

After that unsuccessful endeavor, I downloaded a couple meditation apps on my phone and began the process of "disconnecting." I went into my bedroom, closed the door, surrounded myself with a bunch of pillows, made myself comfortable, and began my meditation practice.

Unfortunately, my family members all found me. One minute into my practice, my daughter knocked on my door with an urgent question. After doing my best to answer and then shooing her out of the room, I got into my comfortable position again. That's when my young son came looking for me. After explaining to him that "Mommy is busy right now," I once again tried to engage in meditation. Two minutes later, my husband found me and wanted to talk.

Before you judge me for having no boundaries, I want you to appreciate the fact that I live with several family members who have ADHD. The moment I am preoccupied, I suddenly become the most fascinating person in the house. After patiently explaining to my husband that this was "my time," I locked the door. Unfortunately, our dog suddenly experienced separation anxiety and started barking outside the bedroom. At that point, I gave up and decided that meditation might not be the best relaxation of choice for me.

About eight years ago, shortly after my failed meditation experiences, I rediscovered my love of tennis. Tennis was a sport I began playing in high school, but I gave it up after graduation. As my daughters grew, they started taking tennis lessons and joined their school tennis teams. After many years as a tennis mom/spectator, I decided I wanted to play again, too.

Reconnecting with this sport has been very therapeutic for me. I initially started by joining a tennis clinic where I made some new "tennis friends." After a few years, I took a risk, joined a team and played doubles. Now, I don't want to misrepresent myself as an amazing player, but through practice I have become an engaged, above average player. More importantly, I've found an outlet for my competitive energy, a release for my racing thoughts, and a place where I can exercise and have fun.

Recently, I became aware of some of the psychological benefits of playing tennis. First and foremost, I realized that when I'm playing a match, I actually use many of the self-soothing techniques I recommend to my patients. For example, I use positive self-talk while playing. I speak to myself in a kind voice and say things like, "You've got this," or, "You can do it." (On a side note, my tennis partner tells me that she appreciates when I say those positive statements aloud to encourage her.) When I feel myself getting anxious before returning a serve, I remind myself to breathe. Just the act of exhaling a deep breath makes me feel calmer.

Additionally, I find that playing in a match helps me stay in the present moment. For example, if there is ever a dispute between players about whether a ball is in bounds or out, or if I make a bad serve, I have learned to let it go. Instead of beating myself up wondering if my opponent is judging me, whether my call was correct, or if my serve was "good enough," I have learned to move on and just focus on the next ball arching toward me from across the net.

My mantra, which I repeat to myself many times during a match, is simple: be present. Additionally, while I am playing, I don't think about my family members, patients, or worries. I just focus on the next ball in front of me.

I have taken this analogy off the tennis courts and into my life. For example, when I am with family and I catch myself thinking about the future or questioning some decision I have made in the past, I try to redirect myself with the mantra: be present. I engage the same strategy when I am counseling patients. Instead of focusing on what my reply to a patient's insight will be, I try to be present and listen to what is being said. Of course, there are times when I'm more successful than others. But either way, I take a moment to commend myself for trying my best to be present.

I have a choice: I can beat myself up for being a meditation flunky, or I can celebrate my resiliency in finding a sport I enjoy that also gives me the benefit of "living in the moment" as meditation does for others. So, if meditation doesn't suit you, don't worry. I encourage you to find an activity that helps you relax and focus on the present moment. Whether it's playing tennis, taking pottery classes, doing needlepoint, or performing in a play, take a risk and find your zen.

An interesting insight occurred during the beginning of COVID quarantine (when I was unable to find my zen through tennis.) I was in my office between teletherapy appointments and I had ten minutes with nothing to do. Even though I had long-labeled myself a meditation flunky, I lay down on the sofa and listened to a ten-minute guided meditation on my iPad. Shockingly, it worked. I left my anxiety behind and felt more relaxed and present afterward.

With that direct experience, I decided that during stressful times, meditation could be another tool in my "tool box." Although I had a fairly rocky start with meditation, my recent experiences have been pretty amazing. My takeaway is this: I am still growing and need to be patient and flexible with myself as I continue to evolve. Additionally, once I let go of the expectation of meditating perfectly, I was able to relax and have some incredible experiences.

LIMIT TIME ON SOCIAL MEDIA

I can't stress strongly enough the importance of limiting time on social media. The National Institute of Health (NIH) published a 2016 study done by the University of Pittsburgh School of Medicine in their *Journal of Depression and Anxiety* that showed more time spent on social media increases the chances of depression. Researchers found that the participants who checked social media most during the week were 2.7 times more likely to experience depression. Additionally, *The Journal of Social and Clinical Psychology* published a similar study concluding that there is a causal link between the use of social media and the negative effects of well-being, in particular, depression and loneliness. One of the researchers, Jordyn Young from the University of Pennsylvania, clarified the study's findings, saying, "What we found is that if you use less social media, you are actually less depressed and less lonely."

In my opinion, all these studies seem pretty obvious. The more time you spend looking at Facebook, Instagram, Snapchat, and Twitter, the worse you are going to feel. Whether it is FOMO (Fear of Missing Out) or just a sense of comparing yourself to all those people who are "living their best lives" (or, at least, trying to make it seem like that is the case,) you will feel less-than. Additionally, all of that time you spend staring at a phone keeps you from being present for the relationships that are actually in your life. Instead of being present, you end up distracted.

Todd and Darrell

Darrell called me to set up an appointment for himself and his husband, Todd. After living in San Francisco for six years, he and Todd had recently moved back to Philadelphia, Todd's hometown, to be closer to family who could help them raise their five-year-old daughter, Natalie. The reason for the call was that Darrell was very angry after learning that Todd was having an "emotional affair" with a former lover, Joe, with whom he had reconnected on Facebook.

What made matters worse was that when Todd and Darrell met, Todd was living with another man in a committed relationship. The other man, Mike, had been Todd's long-term partner and also the lead guitarist in a band for which Darrell played the saxophone in the evenings. The band hung out together frequently and pretty quickly Todd and Darrell developed a close friendship. During this time, Todd began confiding in Darrell about how lonely and unhappy he was in his relationship with Mike. Despite a great deal of guilt and shame, Todd and Darrell began an affair and fell in love. Needless to say, this caused a lot of chaos within the band and Mike was heartbroken. Despite their rocky beginning, Darrell and Todd developed a deep bond, married, and adopted their daughter.

Darrell was the co-owner of a tech company and frequently had to travel and give presentations to organizations all over the country. Todd was a teacher who stopped working when they adopted Natalie in San Francisco. After moving back to Pennsylvania, Todd decided to join his mother selling real estate, even though it was not an ideal job for him, in part because his mother was very outspoken and driven and would often speak to him in a condescending tone of voice. The good part of the job was that the hours were flexible, so Todd could arrange his appointments around Natalie's schedule at her posh private school.

Both Darrell and Todd were lonely in Philadelphia. This was, in some ways, unsurprising. After all, they had left a vibrant gay community in which they were deeply connected to move to the more conservative Philadelphia suburbs, and with that, their network of friends went from huge to almost nonexistent.

When they first came in, Todd, a casually dressed, sandy-haired man wearing glasses, was looking shamefully down at the floor. Initially, he did not even make eye contact with me, as if he were brought in to the principal's office after being in trouble. Darrell, a handsome African American man dressed in an expensive suit, cried openly and said he felt like he was being replaced.

Darrell's fear was understandable, considering he knew how exciting it was to have Todd lavish attention on him as an affair partner. He was sure that Todd was having sex with this man, though Todd adamantly denied that.

Eventually, Todd spoke about how hard the past few years had been for him. He said he felt like a single dad while Darrell had the opportunity to dress up in fabulous suits and stay in fancy hotels.

Darrell defensively said that his travel schedule was not so great and that he got anxious every single time he got on an airplane, and that he only did it for their family. Furthermore, Darrell said it was difficult for him to "reestablish himself in Natalie's world" every time he returned from a business trip.

Frustrated, Todd said, "He gets to be the fun parent who plays music loudly and keeps her up past bedtime. I do all of the work! I am the one who wakes her up in the morning and gets her to school on time. I have to deal with her moodiness and help her do all her homework." At this point, I couldn't help but ask, "She has homework in kindergarten?" Suddenly the tension was broken. We all laughed about the ridiculous demands on kids today and how this fancy private school expected even kindergartners to complete homework assignments.

With the tension broken, we talked about how hard parenting is for everyone these days—especially a gay biracial couple doing their best to adjust to a new culture. We also laughed about bossy mothers and how hard it was asking others for help with childcare. Todd apologized for flirting with Joe online and having him over to their house to reconnect. He knew he was entering dangerous territory and how damaging this was for his and Darrell's relationship. Darrell accepted his apology and apologized himself for being angry and moody so frequently.

For a few moments, both Todd and Darrell had stopped defending their own positions and had been truly present to listen to each other's voice. The laughter had caused them to slow down and breathe. It reduced some shame and allowed them to look into each other's eyes and see the pain there.

We were just getting started in our couple's therapy, of course, and had a lot of work ahead of us, including establishing boundaries around social media, addressing their power dynamics, and working through guilt around the beginning of their relationship. We also needed to work on building their communication skills.

Individually, Todd still needed to look at how when his needs were unmet, instead of taking a risk and communicating his pain directly, he would seek validation from an outside source. His pattern of flirtation and affairs was an unhealthy way of fulfilling his desire for attention. We also discussed how he needed to find work outside his mother's real estate firm. For his part, Darrell needed to address his feelings of resentment about no longer having the outlet of playing the saxophone in a band, as well as his anxiety about traveling for work. It was also crucial for Darrell and Todd as a couple to establish roots in the gay community of Philadelphia.

Once we established our treatment goals, Darrell and Todd made quick progress. Although there was a great deal of hurt and betrayal to work through, there was also a lot of love there—love that was most apparent when they were able to step away from their individual agendas and hear each other.

EXERCISE 1

Figure out what activity you have in your life that keeps you present in the moment. Is it a sport, an artistic endeavor, gourmet cooking? Give yourself permission to participate in this activity.

EXERCISE 2

Give yourself permission to imperfectly practice meditation, yoga, or relaxation. Allow this to be a judgment-free time. Start slowly with the goal of ten minutes per day. Gently increase your time if you are feeling the benefits.

8

BOUNDARIES

WHAT ARE BOUNDARIES?

When you expect your partner to be perfect, you believe that he or she will be "perfectly attuned" to your needs and wants. Unfortunately, relationships do not work that way. No one automatically knows what you desire in a relationship. You must communicate your needs. In other words, we must teach people how to treat us. It can be as simple as telling your partner what you expect in a particular situation. For example, saying, "I work hard all week and like to have something to look forward to on the weekends like a date night on Saturdays." Or, "We spent Thanksgiving with your extended family, let's spend Christmas with mine."

Instead of assuming that your partner has the same desires as you, it is important to speak up about what you want. When you fail to speak up assertively, resentments may begin. Speaking up for yourself also establishes basic guidelines for how you want to be treated and allows your partner to do the same. This is called setting boundaries. Boundaries are basic guidelines that we create to establish how others

At the same time, this client and I worked together on setting some boundaries, which included limiting her phone calls to her mother to one fifteen-minute call on Sundays. And when her mother would begin her excessive complaining, my patient would simply listen without trying to offer help or would change the subject. When my patient stopped being her mother's surrogate psychologist, her mother was forced to hire an actual therapist and their relationship finally improved.

One of the costs of taking on a caretaker role in childhood is that it impacts your adult relationships. You may get overwhelmed when hearing a friend's problems and try too hard to heal that person. You might also avoid the friendship altogether. You may be picking emotionally needy relationships that remind you of your parent's drama. You may also unconsciously try to recreate situations from your childhood in order to fix your relationships, such as picking a partner who is always in crisis so you can be the rescuer. The more you work on your awareness of your childhood dynamics, the easier it will be to free yourself from drama.

ENMESHMENT

Another type of boundary violation that impacts interpersonal relationships is when one of the partners remains enmeshed with his or her parent. The concept of enmeshment was first introduced by Salvador Minuchin in the 1970s. It refers to a situation where family members are close to an extent that it becomes difficult for each member to establish a healthy level of independence. Examples could include:

- A lack of appropriate privacy between parent and child.
- A child becoming "best friends" with a parent.
- A parent confiding secrets to a child.
- A parent becoming overly involved in the child's activities.

Often, a parent's lack of boundaries places the child in the uncomfortable position of being the parent's surrogate spouse. The following example, Tim and Joey's story, illustrates how parental enmeshment can impact a partner's ability to be present in a romantic relationship.

Tim and Joey

Tim and Joey had a beautiful relationship. They had been together for over three years and were planning to marry the following summer. They had met while working in a high-end department store and were fashionable as well as hardworking. They viewed each other as kindred spirits. Both had eccentric senses of style and wicked senses of humor.

After they began dating, Tim left retail to work for a famous celebrity chef who was opening a restaurant in Philadelphia. The trendy restaurant was extremely successful and Tim proved to be invaluable to his boss. He was so impressed with how Tim ran the restaurant that he asked him to relocate to Los Angeles so they could open another place.

Tim was elated and couldn't wait to share his opportunity with Joey. When Joey heard about the idea of relocating, he was also thrilled. It was both of their dream to live in a vibrant fashion forward city that had a robust gay community. Tim loved the restaurant scene and Joey envisioned himself becoming a professional fashion stylist for the stars. There was only one problem: Joey's mother.

The reason that Tim and Joey were in therapy was that they were scared to tell Joey's mother that they wanted to move. Tim and Joey lived together in a row house in South Philadelphia directly next door to Joey's mother, Mary Theresa. Mary Theresa had made Joey her surrogate husband since the day his dad died 19 years earlier. She would call Joey at least 5 or 6 times a day. The first calls often before 8 a.m., began with the question, "You up?"

As the day proceeded, Mary Theresa would Facetime Joey for advice on what to wear, and then call him several more times to complain about his sisters. She would also ask Joey for help whenever she had a computer problem or wanted to have furniture moved in her home.

Although her requests were sometimes tedious, there were perks about having her close, as she was a great cook of Italian food and would often deliver a platter of meatballs or pasta to them at the end of the day.

Tim realized that there were good aspects to Mary Theresa, such as how accepting she was of Joey's gay lifestyle, despite the fact that she was raised Catholic. She had embraced his choice of Tim as a partner and was generous and loving to them both. However, she did not respect their boundaries and would frequently call them or stop over with "emergencies." Her lack of boundaries was upsetting to Tim, who felt like she was constantly intruding upon their time alone.

Tim had been patient and supportive of Mary Theresa from the start, but enough was enough. Her behaviors were driving Tim crazy, but unfortunately Joey wasn't changing anything in their relationship. Each day, Joey promised to tell his mother about the move, but then he would change his mind.

"It's his job to set boundaries with his mother," said Tim, "not mine. We're supposed to be in California in 30 days and she still doesn't have a clue." Joey shrugged his shoulders, then began to explain how hard it was growing up in the tightly knit Italian family he was born into. When he was a child, his mother had been his protector against his homophobic father and the other children in the neighborhood who didn't understand his differences. True, she did lean on him a lot, but, as she put it, she was "all alone in this world."

Mary Theresa had used guilt to keep Joey close to her physically as well as emotionally. He had been taking care of his mother's needs since he was a little boy, even before his emotionally absent father died. His father had worked long hours as a construction foreman, and when he came home, he would rarely have energy left for his wife or children. Mary Theresa would confide to Joey about how lonely she was and frustrated with her husband's quick temper and inability to meet her needs. She would even complain to Joey about their lack of a sex life, which would make Joey feel very uncomfortable. "Thank God I have you," she would say, as she complained about his father and her conflictual relationship with his two sisters.

When Tim and Joey first came in for couples therapy, I realized the precariousness of the situation. We had to move quickly since they were planning to relocate in less than a month. Joey shared with me his internal struggle as he didn't want to devastate his mom but he also wanted to live his own life and pursue his dreams with his future husband. He told me he was aware of his role as his mother's partner and was ready to resign from that position.

I recommended that they both begin reading about enmeshment issues and suggested Kenneth Adams' books, *Silently Seduced* and *When He's Married to Mom*. Additionally, we created a script about how he could directly tell his mother that he was planning to move. Tim role-played with him and responded the way that he believed Mary Theresa might react. To his credit, Joey was able to handle any response that Tim expressed. He also practiced setting limits on how often he and his mother would communicate while they both adjusted to his moving away.

Joey found the books extremely helpful and became aware of how his lack of setting boundaries with his mother had contributed to his struggles with intimacy in his relationship with Tim. At times, he was not present to listen to Tim because he was too overwhelmed by his mother's neediness. He had also stunted his own growth by not moving out of his South Philly neighborhood. Having his mother as his next-door neighbor had also kept him from feeling independent.

When Joey told Mary Theresa that he was moving to California, her first reaction was hysterics. She cried and asked him who would be there for her? When he didn't abandon his plan and kept consistent with his practiced script, she calmed down and listened to what he said about pursuing his dreams. Joey reassured her that they would stay close but it was his time to give more energy to his romantic relationship and his career.

Over the next several therapy sessions, Joey and Tim worked on being a unified couple as they lovingly detached from Mary Theresa and focused on moving to California. Although the transition wasn't easy for Joey, he sent me a sunny post card several months after the move to let me know that they had settled in and he was glad that they had relocated. The postcard even had a P.S. telling me that Mary Theresa was adjusting, too.

PRACTICAL TIPS WHEN SETTING BOUNDARIES

The acronym HALT (for Hungry, Angry, Lonely, Tired) is a useful guideline to use when you are setting boundaries. What I mean by this is that you should never try to set or implement a boundary when you are feeling hungry, angry, lonely, or tired. When you are feeling depleted, your words will have much less conviction and you will be less clear on your intentions. Healthy conversations and boundary setting work better once you have taken care of your own needs.

So, if you are hungry, indulge in a satisfying meal before you have to do the difficult task of setting boundaries. If you are feeling angry, journal about your feelings first so your resentments do not impact your communication. If you are feeling lonely, reach out to a friend or a supportive person and discuss your feelings before you set the boundaries. Additionally, make sure that you are well rested before you attempt to implement boundaries. Taking care of yourself first puts you in a much better position to set limits with other people.

You can practice setting boundaries before you actually set them. In the previous example, Joey role-played what he was going to say to his mother before he attempted the difficult conversation with her. You can practice by role-playing with your therapist, partner, family member, or friend. Writing out your script in advance is another way to become clear on the boundary or boundaries that you want to implement. The objective is to be comfortable with whatever resistance arises.

EXERCISE 1

Develop a list of three boundaries that you would like to implement in your relationship. Ask your partner to do the same. Share your lists of boundaries and communicate together how you can fine-tune them so that they can work for your relationship.

EXERCISE 2

Sit down with your partner and develop a list of three boundaries that you would like to implement with your extended family. Figure out a plan to effectively communicate these boundaries with your family members.

9

WHEN WE LOSE OUR WAY

NAVIGATING LIFE'S WRONG TURNS

I am directionally challenged. In the past, I got overwhelmed by maps and needed to write out my directions in words, including as many landmarks as possible so it would make sense to me and I wouldn't end up lost. From my perspective, one of the greatest inventions of all time is navigation systems for cars and phones. Instead of having to fumble with maps and directions from strangers, I can just follow my Waze app.

In therapy sessions, I often share with patients my belief that the navigation system I use in my car is a great analogy for life. I explain that there are times while driving, even with this wonderful navigation system, that I blow it. I miss the turn completely, or I turn left when the app says to turn right. What I love about the navigation system is that it does not judge me, it just tells me how to correct my course. The navigation system does not say to me, "You screwed up, you stupid idiot!" Instead, it says, "in a quarter mile turn right." There is no cruelty, sarcasm, or judgment. It simply tells me to do the next right thing.

Twelve-step fellowships have been promoting this "do the next right thing" slogan for years, and it is one of the principles I try to follow as I live my life. Instead of beating myself up for making choices that were not exactly in line with my highest self, I just keep showing up and trying to do better. Whether I overreact as a parent or communicate too harshly to a friend, I concentrate on breathing, and on slowly letting go of the harsh voice in my head that is judging me. I try to quiet that critical voice and focus on compassion and self-forgiveness. When that doesn't work, I just try to do the next right thing.

THE HEALING POWER OF NATURE

When I am struggling with life's inevitable traumas, losses, or disappointments I spend time in nature. I am a big proponent of taking hikes, spending time in gardens, and watching sunsets. It reminds me that my pain is just a small part of a spectacular world.

On February 23, 1944, Anne Frank, a well-known diarist and victim of the Holocaust, wrote in her diary, "The best remedy for those who are afraid, lonely, or unhappy is to go outside somewhere where they can be alone with the heavens, nature, and God." She urged others to "go outside…amidst the simple beauty of nature and know that as long as places like this exist, there will be comfort for every sorrow, whatever the circumstance may be."

One of my colleagues spends hours gardening. Her happy place involves digging in the dirt and creating beauty out of bare soil. For me, I find solace walking in a wooded area by the creek near my house with my dog, Rosie. Each season provides an incredible landscape for my thoughts. There are many different ways to incorporate nature into your healing, regardless of the weather.

NATURE PROVIDES ME AN OASIS

Many years ago, after going through a stressful period in my marriage, I looked outside and the March sky was gray and gloomy, which reflected my mood. My husband suggested that we spend the day at the Philadelphia Flower Show.

We had been bickering that morning and I was not particularly excited to spend the day with him, but I agreed to go. The Philadelphia Flower Show has always held a special significance for me because it reminds me of my grandmother, who would take me there when I was a small child.

Once we arrived, my husband and I were transported into a glorious alternative world of flowers and beautiful landscapes. The majestic displays took us out of our own perspectives and showed us something outside of ourselves. By the time we left the flower show, our disagreement seemed a bit more removed as we had come together to experience the wonder of beauty in the world. Additionally, I felt more connected with my grandmother, who had endured many difficult moments in her marriage but still had managed to live a good life.

THE MESSAGES WE TELL OURSELVES

Sometimes we get in our own way and block our growth as well as the growth of our relationships. As human beings, our goal is to evolve and not simply repeat the past. The messages we tell ourselves are crucial and either keep us stuck in the past or promote growth for the future.

NEGATIVE MESSAGES

Before you can heal your relationships, you need to heal yourself. Almost every self-help book ever written describes the concept of learning to love yourself. This is easier said than done. We all have a lifetime of negative messages that we play on repeat. These are messages that we may have heard explicitly from parents, siblings, or peers pointing out what is wrong with us.

It could be etched in our brain when we are ridiculed by a classmate or screamed at by a frustrated parent. It could also be implicitly taught to us through actions, such as if we are frequently picked last for a team in gym class or fail our science tests despite studying. These messages may say that we are unathletic or stupid or simply not good enough. I am a practical person who needs concrete methods of challenging those negative messages. One of my favorite strategies to combat negative messages is to create the opposite truth in the form of a mantra.

MANTRAS

A wonderful example of a mantra is illustrated in the 2011 film, *The Help*. A young girl in the film, Mae Mobley, is neglected by her socialite mother. In an attempt to challenge the negative impact of what the girl is living through, the black maid, Aibileen Clark, who is raising Mae, would say, "You is kind. You is smart. You is important." Aibileen wants to increase the young girl's self-esteem by letting her know that she matters. The repetition of those words over and over again soothes Mae Mobley and serves as a building block for the confidence she later develops as an adult.

Our negative self-talk is composed of the many critical statements we received as children, along with how we interpreted the criticism. When our adult experiences reinforce the negative messages, the voices get louder. It is up to us to quiet the voices by challenging them with positive messages. For example, if a young girl is neglected by her par-

ents, she grows up thinking she is not worthy of a meaningful relationship. If later on she selects a partner who is a workaholic, her childhood
message becomes reinforced. Another example is when a little boy is
verbally abused by his mother and told that he will never amount to
anything. He may end up choosing a partner who is extremely critical of
him, which will reinforce his belief that he is not good enough.

The work of therapy is to challenge negative beliefs that are not true.
The act of creating a mantra retrains your brain to believe positive attributes about yourself. One of the mantras I use when I feel incompetent
is, "I've got this. I can do it." My young son has heard me say this and
rolls his eyes in a humorous way of communicating, "There is my mom
talking to herself again." Even if I do look silly when I speak to myself
aloud, it actually works. Positive self-talk is essential to building self-esteem and challenging those moments of doubt.

I often have patients write down their mantras and repeat them frequently to themselves. Their mantra can attack a specific shameful belief,
perhaps something like:

- I am beautiful.
- I am smart.
- I am courageous.

The mantra might also be targeted to a specific situation, such as,
I will get through this and live an incredible life.

The following story about Emily illustrates the impact of negative
messages and the value of creating positive mantras to alter your personal narrative.

Emily

Emily was a college senior who came into my office for therapy at the recommendation of her mother's treatment center.
Her mother was in rehab again. This was the fifth time in the

past ten years that her mother had relapsed from alcoholism. Emily did not want to get her hopes up that her mother was going to "get it" this time. In fact, Emily said in her first session that she was not here to talk about her mother's problems. Instead, she wanted to talk about her own.

Emily was a beautiful African American woman with dark eyes, long black hair, and a flawless complexion. She was having a difficult time getting along with her roommates, who were often cruel to her. She believed that they talked behind her back and excluded her from their plans.

Emily also wanted to explore why she kept making disastrous choices with men. During her first year of college, she had occasionally gone out drinking with friends and woken up in different boys' dorm rooms with no memory of even meeting them. In one of these incidents, she had contracted a venereal disease. This had devastated Emily, and she would say things to herself like:

- I'm damaged goods.
- No decent guy will ever like me.
- I'm unlovable.
- Once anyone gets to know me, I will just be rejected.

The truth was that Emily was incredibly lovable. She was extremely smart, creative, and beautiful. But her self-esteem was terrible. The negative messages she began telling herself as a little girl dealing with her mother's alcoholism had gotten louder and louder after she made some bad decisions in college. As an only child, Emily felt very alone coping with her mother's issues and didn't have anyone with whom she felt safe confiding her college struggles.

Her relationship with her mother was complicated. When

her mother was sober, they got along very well. But whenever her mother would relapse, her behavior would completely change and she would be unreliable and cruel. She would call Emily a disappointment and tell her that she should never have had her. This would devastate Emily. In fact, in high school Emily began cutting herself and even attempted suicide as she told herself, "I don't deserve to live."

College was supposed to be a fresh start for Emily, and in some ways, she was thriving. Academically, she was incredibly accomplished. She was an English major who was brilliant in understanding characters' plights in novels. She was also involved in many activist groups on campus including environmental causes, political awareness groups, gay rights, and a feminist club. She was a sensitive person actively working to help make other people's lives better, but her own life was still a challenge.

In therapy we addressed the depression Emily had been living with, and we worked on increasing her coping skills—adding journaling, exercise, and more general forms of self-care. She also began taking an antidepressant to address some of the symptoms of depression that were impairing her daily functioning such as waking up early in the morning, not having an appetite, and feeling worthless. In time, she started feeling better.

Over the year that Emily came in for counseling, she changed her physical appearance many times. She cut her hair really short one week. The next week she dyed it lavender. Emily was experimenting with who she wanted to be. She got several more tattoos. An interesting thing happened while Emily was getting a colorful butterfly tattooed on her ankle. She began talking to the tattoo artist Patrick, who was a recent graduate from art school.

She explained to him that the butterfly symbolized all of the change she was experiencing and that she was in therapy now and committed to her metamorphosis. Patrick listened attentively and when he was finished asked for her phone number.

Emily came to see me the following week and shared how Patrick had called her and they had gone on a twelve-hour date. They had gone to an old-fashioned diner with a jukebox and had eaten ice cream sundaes, listened to music, and laughed for hours. Then they walked holding hands throughout the city.

Emily was visibly shaken. She really liked this guy. He was gentle and kind and seemed to actually listen to what she had to say. She was scared because she did not feel worthy of a man this good. The guys that she had hooked up with before seemed much more into satisfying their own needs as opposed to getting to know her. She did not want to get too excited and told me that she was "waiting for the other shoe to drop." Still, Patrick had called her after their marathon first date and asked her out again the night after our therapy session.

Emily shared with me that she was used to people disappointing her, and even her roommates had let her down. We discussed her role in this phenomenon and how she tended to select people in her life who were similar to her mom by being unreliable and only kind to her sometimes.

We also began to unpack some of the negative messages that she told herself, including that she was bad and not worth anyone good loving her. We decided to challenge some of those messages and she created a short series of mantras:

I am a good person and I deserve other good people in my life.

I am loveable and filled with light.

I am worthy of love, intimacy, and connection.

She wrote these mantras down and promised to hang them next to her mirror in her room. She also promised to remain open to getting to know Patrick, and vowed not to sabotage their date that evening.

The following week Emily came in smiling. She had spent several nights that week with Patrick and admitted she felt even more connected with him. They had talked about being sexual and she told me how ashamed she was to share with him that she had a sexually transmitted disease but had wanted to be honest. He handled it beautifully, and they agreed to practice safe sex whenever she felt ready to trust him. Within several weeks they had developed a healthy sex life as well as a communicative emotional relationship.

Eventually, Emily shared with Patrick some of her pain about her relationship with her mother. He held her while she cried. Through this corrective emotional experience, she began to gain more acceptance of herself.

Over the next six months of Emily's therapy, she continued to blossom in this healthy relationship. Patrick's unconditional love and gentle, unassuming manner helped her gain confidence in herself. She continued to repeat her mantras and, over time, decided to move out of her apartment and away from her judgmental roommates. She moved in with another young woman whom she had met in one of her classes, Anna, who was accepting and kind.

Emily ended her therapy with me when she graduated college. Although I knew I was going to miss her, I was glad to be replaced by the supportive relationships she now had with Anna and Patrick.

IF YOU ARE STRUGGLING TO COME UP WITH A MANTRA, BORROW ONE

As a child of the 70s, I was influenced, and at times rescued, by rock music. For whatever problem I was struggling with, I tended to find a song that would resonate. A song that truly impacted me was written by an English rock band called Argent. The catchy title and chorus felt like a healing mantra that I have always held on to, "Hold Your Head Up." I would repeat that before I even knew what the term mantra meant.

Another mantra that I borrowed from a song was written by the great Sir Elton John. The title and chorus is simply, "I'm Still Standing." No matter what happens, this mantra reminds me of my endurance, strength, and perseverance. I have shared both of these examples of mantras with patients to encourage them to either come up with their own, to borrow mine, or to find a song lyric that speaks to them.

WISDOM LEARNED FROM SPIN CLASS

For the past 25 years, one of my favorite ways to exercise has been to attend spin classes. I love the energy of a group of fellow biking enthusiasts getting together for one hour in a small room while the music blasts with a common goal of burning as many calories and getting as physically fit as possible. It also feels time-efficient to me. Plus, 60 minutes to leave all my stress behind on a bike seems like a good deal.

Years ago, I used to belong to a gym called LA Fitness. There were two different spin instructors that stood out to me. One was a young muscular woman whose name I can't recall. I'll just refer to her as "The Satan of Spin" She was famous at the gym for pushing her classes extremely hard and could be heard saying comments to the participants like "What is the matter with you?" "Are you lazy?" "You suck." "Is that all you've got?" "You are slow and out of shape The Satan of Spin would walk close to someone on a bike and then scream disparaging comments in that person's face. The intent was to push each of us to get the best workout we could. The problem was that even if we accomplished good workouts, we would all leave the class feeling demoralized.

Contrasting with The Satan of Spin was an instructor named Jack. Jack must have been in his early 70s. His 8 a.m. Sunday morning class was so popular that the participants would arrive 30 minutes before the gym even opened, lining up outside in the hope that they would get a bike. The party would start in the parking lot as we all enthusiastically waited for Jack's class.

Jack was one of the most positive and inspiring instructors that I had ever had. He would select uplifting music with motivating messages and would walk up to the cyclists in his class and make comments such as "Today is the day." "You are beautiful and strong." "You can do anything." "Look how powerful you are!" As a result, we would push ourselves hard and accomplish great workouts. More importantly, we would walk out of that class feeling like a million bucks. After we were fed so many positive, nourishing comments, we would leave that class and carry the positivity all day.

All of these years later, my takeaway from this gym experience is that there are two different ways to motivate ourselves: feeding the harsh judgmental voice of our inner critic, or choosing to nourish ourselves by taking in inspirational, loving messages. We have many choices in our lives. We can choose to surround ourselves with critical/judgmental people or we can select individuals who see the good in us. I advocate for the second option. We all need "atta-boys" or "atta-girls." We need to know that others see our goodness in us and how hard we are trying.

VISUALIZATIONS

Sometimes when we are struggling or feeling alone, a visualization can help. The following example describes a visualization I have used with patients who are feeling lost or confused about their next course of action.

Who Sits at the Table in Your Boardroom?

"Who sits at the table in your boardroom?" I asked my handsome, elegantly dressed 40-something patient. He looked at me with a confused expression. He was a man in recovery from an addiction who was struggling with some difficult relationship decisions. He is similar to many of the high-functioning executives I counsel, and he was not sure if I was referring to the boardroom for the financial organization where he works, or if I was looking for a deeper meaning. It was the latter, of course.

I told him to close his eyes and take several deep breaths. When he seemed in a more relaxed state of mind, I asked him to visualize himself in a beautiful boardroom. I described a long table circled by comfortable chairs and told him this was the table set aside for his executive board of personal advisors. I let him know that he could fill these chairs with the most important and trusted people in his life. I told him that not everyone at that table needs to be someone he sees frequently. In fact, not even everyone at that table even needs to be alive.

As we did this visualization, I gave him several moments to picture the individuals he wanted at his table. Who could give him the most support or guidance? The chairs could be filled with anyone he had ever met, but I hoped they would be filled with people who cared about him and loved him deeply.

After several minutes of this visualization, I asked him to picture himself looking around the table at each of the people sitting in the chairs and to greet them. I suggested that he look in their eyes and welcome them to his boardroom and ask, "Is there anything you want to tell me? Is there any advice, suggestion, or support you could share?"

After he greeted each person individually and listened to that person's words of advice, I asked him to imagine looking in each of their eyes and saying goodbye. This was a moment where he could thank each person for his or her contribution and tell them that he would call them back in the future if he needed their support again. After completing this visualization, I gave him a moment to open his eyes and orient himself back into the therapy room.

As my patient looked around the room, I realized that his eyes were filled with tears. He shared with me that this was a powerful exercise for him, and he'd pictured people who were both living and dead. He told me that I was sitting at his table, at the head opposite him. I replied that I was honored. He also told me that there was a chair occupied by his old high school basketball coach who believed in him at a time in his life when he felt very alone. His recovery sponsor was in a chair rooting for him as he spoke in his usual blunt manner. His deceased father was there imparting his words of wisdom. Additionally, his college friend who now lives on the West Coast made an appearance. His middle school English teacher was there along with a favorite aunt who had died way too early. He pictured two of his recovery friends also sitting at the table.

I have done this visualization exercise with many of my patients. I have also created my own advisory board. One of the things I love about this exercise is that it reminds us we are not alone; however, it is contradictory to traditional psychotherapy, where there is one all-knowing doctor who treats a suffering patient. The advisory board exercise supports my belief that we all need a team to support us.

Whether the members of our board are living or not, we have guides. It is up to us to listen to them.

For this patient, his advisory board helped him with a difficult decision he needed to make. After that session I encouraged him to imagine that his table can be with him whenever he is struggling. All he has to do is visualize his team right there with him and he will feel less alone.

WHAT ABOUT GOD?

I remember going to a training for therapists in Arizona many years ago. The speaker was an older gentleman with a commanding presence, dressed in pure Southwestern style complete with cowboy boots and a hat. His voice bellowed out to us as he said, "There's only one thing that you need to know about God." There was a pause in his drawl as all of the therapists in the room leaned in, poised with our pens in our hands, ready to write down whatever words of wisdom he provided. "You ain't Him." That moment has always stuck with me. When we are trying to look for perfection in our partners, we are trying to control what we believe they should be. We are taking on God's role.

It is helpful when you are stuck in your relationships and are unsure what to do that you look toward a power greater than yourself to help you. The good news here is that you don't have to perfectly understand God in order to believe in a power greater than yourself. You only must believe that you will need and accept outside help. This could mean that even if you struggle with a traditional version of God, you will look for supportive real-world people who could aid you in your moment of crisis, including therapists, 12-step fellowships, 12-step sponsors, and trustworthy friends. God could become an acronym for "Good Orderly Direction" given by your advisors and spiritual network.

For people who have a good working relationship with religion or spiritual practices, praying or asking your higher power for help makes all the sense in the world. For others, the religion of their early life is simply too ingrained and the resentments run too deep. An exercise is provided at the end of this chapter to help you if you are struggling to develop a loving relationship with your higher power.

What I love about looking toward my higher power for help is that I often feel less alone. I feel comforted believing in a force greater than myself. In general, I believe in a team approach to life whenever possible, as opposed to acting as if I have all the answers. My belief in a higher power is just an extension of that.

FEAR OF TRUSTING OTHERS

Many of us grew up in families where we received the message that we have to handle everything by ourselves. If we want to appear perfect, we do not need to ask for help from anyone. While doing this, we learn not to let other people see our inadequacies. We hide and do not risk exposing our uncertainty to others. The problem with this strategy is that we miss out on an opportunity to be truly seen by others and to gain support.

PUTTING ON A FALSE FRONT

When I was in my early twenties, I went through a tumultuous breakup with a boyfriend I thought I was going to marry. I was sad. At the time, I was in graduate school and working at a community mental health center. I loved my work at the center, and I was grateful to be able to distract myself from the pain I was feeling in order to be of service for our many patients, most of whom desperately needed our help.

One day on my lunch break, I shared with a colleague how much I was struggling with sadness since my boyfriend and I had separated. He looked at me and said, "You, sad? How can that be? You are always so together and well accessorized." This comment still makes me laugh. I was raised in a family where we were taught to look good. Like many alcoholic families, we always presented a great image. No matter what was happening in my life, I learned to get up, wash my face, and put on lipstick. This is the perfectionist's mantra. Never let them see you sweat.

Later that day, one of my patients described his alcoholic family at the dinner table. He told me that they could be fighting brutally with insults being flung harshly at each other, and then the phone would ring. His mother would rise from the table and put on her most cheery voice and say, "Hello," as if she did not have a care in the world.

When we learn to put on a false front, we distance ourselves from our pain. We stuff our emotions and deny even ourselves the opportunity to process our feelings. These pushed down feelings lead to depression, anxiety, and relationship problems.

It is OK to admit you are having struggles and have lost your way. You do not need to appear to be perfect. When you reveal that you are struggling, you give others the gift and the opportunity to be there for you. Whether you are experiencing difficulties in your relationship or feeling lost within yourself, the more you share with your support system, the more you allow them the opportunity to provide assistance, love, and care for you. Additionally, the more genuine you are in your disclosure with your friends, the more they will share their authentic selves with you.

EXERCISE 1

Describe your concept of support and what self-care looks like for you. Journal about ways you can expand your support network. Who are you willing to add?

EXERCISE 2

List the people in your boardroom, with a brief statement about what they have to say to you, and why they are there.

EXERCISE 3

The God Circle: this is an exercise I learned about through the writing of Scott Brassart and Kristen Snowden in their book *Life Anonymous: 12 Steps to Heal and Transform Your Life*.

First, get a large sheet of paper and draw a big circle on it. Inside that circle, list attributes you want and need from your Higher Power. Probably you will come up with things like loving, caring, honest, funny, and nurturing, plus a few others. You can also clip images from magazines or elsewhere that represent these traits in ways that are meaningful to you. Then, paste those images in the circle. Next, do the same thing with undesirable traits—angry, judgmental, punishing, controlling etc.—but write those words and paste the images outside the circle.

Next, use a pair of scissors to cut away the traits and any additional space until all that is left is a perfect circle. Rip up those undesirable traits. You can have a ceremony and burn them or dispose of them in some other way.

Finally, take the remaining circle and put it where you will see it several times each day. As you do this, think about your higher power and how it is represented by the traits and images in the circle. If you need to, act as though this is your understanding of your higher power, even if you don't yet believe it. Do this for 30 days and see how your thoughts evolve.

EXERCISE 4

What is the false front you put on for the world to see? Who are you underneath that false front? Draw a picture of the false front you show to the world. On the other side of the piece of paper, draw who you really are. Look at the contrast between the two sides of the paper. Have compassion for yourself for the mask that you needed to wear. Now, make a proactive decision about those with whom will share your authentic side. Begin by selecting one safe friend or family member who you can be vulnerable with and share your drawing. Over time, expand your ability to trust and share your drawing with another person.

10

CORONAVIRUS LESSONS

WE MAKE PLANS AND GOD LAUGHS

We make plans and God laughs at us. 2020 taught me that. 2020 was supposed to be my summer of writing. My youngest child was going away to summer camp, so, for the first time since I had my first child, all three kids would be out of the house for an extended period of time.

I envisioned having "me time." I pictured myself wearing a lot of sundresses and laughing while I sat with my husband at outdoor cafes without a care in the world. I envisioned myself very intellectually stimulated and motivated to go home after these marathon dinner dates and let all my ideas flow. I pictured myself taking time off from seeing patients and letting my ideas come to fruition. What I have learned, time and time again, is that life does not go according to plan.

In March of 2020, the coronavirus hit. What that meant for me was that all three kids were home—all the time. My oldest came home from college when classes moved online, and my two younger children were suddenly supposed to be home-schooled. Added to this was the fact that my therapy practice had never been busier. The whole world felt traumatized by losses and I found myself working around the clock while also trying to help keep my family members safe and educated. At the same time, my elderly parents were scared to death and needed me to bring them food and to check in with them on a daily basis.

My fantasy of "me time" was simply not going to happen. How interesting that in writing a book about perfectionism, I could not even find a perfect time to write! Both my practice and my family life were changing. There was so much beyond my control. Instead of advising my children about what their next academic decision should be, I just became a witness to their process. Instead of focusing on typical couple's therapy topics with my patients, I was simply helping each person deal with all of the losses and limitations that were in their way.

As a therapist, I was powerless regarding health struggles and the deaths that COVID-19 was causing. All I could do was be honest. I shared my own vulnerability, sadness, and anxiety. As I helped lead the way for my patients, I also became aware of how much growth we were all experiencing. In a time of tremendous loss, there was also beauty and magic as we became aware of what was really important in our lives.

LOVE IN THE TIME OF CORONAVIRUS

My 30-year-old patient just told me he recently asked a woman he met on Hinge, "Would you rather go on a first date through: FaceTime, Zoom, or scream at each other from 6 feet away in a park?" Being quarantined home alone in his apartment reminded him of his deep desire to develop a healthy relationship.

For others, especially those who were already in intimate relationships and living together, quarantine felt like the ultimate stress test. In fact, there has been research looking at how people cope after tragic life events. In 2002, *The Journal of Family Psychology* produced a paper after Hurricane Hugo looking at how people in devastated counties of South Carolina coped after this tragedy. In this paper, the authors explained how attachment theorists would predict more marriages and births. Stress researchers on the other hand, predicted that marriages and births would decline and divorces would increase.

What actually happened in the year after Hurricane Hugo was that they both were right. There was an increase in marriages as well as births, and there was also an increase in divorces. What this showed was that life-threatening events motivate people to take significant actions in their lives. What this could mean for us, as I write this chapter in the time of COVID-19, is that crises of all types present a crucial time for people to take stock of their lives and realize what is really important.

For people who are consumed with work, being home full-time gives them the opportunity to focus on their relationships with family. Although there is a great deal of good in this, it can also be stressful. Add in the additional pressure of financial uncertainty, fear about getting sick and losing the ones we love, and the fact that there is no end in sight to this virus (at this time, anyway), and even the smallest struggles can feel huge. We are all experiencing grief as we cope with the various losses in our lives.

As a clinical psychologist who usually spends my days counseling individuals and couples face-to-face in my office, I have had to change my practice. I now conduct many of my therapy sessions through FaceTime, phone calls, or Zoom sessions. As people get more and more anxious, I find myself working harder and longer hours. I am more tired and depleted as a result. Still, upon reflection, I have learned a lot of useful information through this time, and I would like to share what I have learned with you so that your relationships do not suffer through this time of COVID-19 and beyond.

WHAT I HAVE LEARNED COUNSELING COUPLES DURING COVID-19 THROUGH FACETIME, ZOOM, AND PHONE SESSIONS

Tone of Voice

Tone of voice is everything. How something is said, not just what is said, matters. During my phone sessions, I am much more focused on the way information is stated. Without the distraction of looking at someone, I am able to really notice the pauses between words and how forceful people can be in their communication style. I can literally feel the other person distancing when the communication style is harsh. This reminds me of the significance of modulating my own voice when speaking to my family members. Letting go of the intenseness of our communication may allow us to be heard in a gentler yet more meaningful way.

Changing Your Praise to Criticism Ratio

According to Dr. John Gottman's research, for a relationship to stay together there need to be five positive remarks to each negative remark. While you are home spending more time with your partner, it is easy to focus on what is bothering you. Make a conscious effort to instead point out what you appreciate. "Thank you for taking our children for a walk so I could get some work done. I am glad that you are so connected with nature and able to teach our children to value it, too."

Gratitude is Essential

In a time of loss, it is important to focus on what we still have.

Before each of my FaceTime, Zoom, or phone sessions, I spend a moment thinking about each person I am going to meet. I focus on something I am grateful for because of our relationship. For example, I reflect on the woman who had the strength to leave her abusive relationship before the time of quarantine. I am so grateful she is safe now. She taught me to not waver on your own convictions and the value of being brave. I am also grateful for the man who got into recovery one month before the quarantine and is now using online 12-step meetings. He has taught me the value of persistence.

Along with being grateful for each of the wonderful people I am able to counsel, I am also grateful for the little things, like having a good cup of my favorite hazelnut coffee and having a bright and beautiful office to sit in while I do my counseling. I am also extremely grateful for my white fluffy dog, Rosie, who is always up for a walk.

If expressing gratitude does not come easily to you, begin with a gratitude journal or a moment of meditation where you focus on the awareness of one thing you are grateful for.

The Value of Touch

The coronavirus time of social distancing has decreased our ability to take and give touch, handshakes, and hugs. It is so important to affirm the people you are living with by touching them, holding hands, and snuggling up. We are all scared in this uncertain time, and touch is an important way to help soothe yourself and others.

Eye Contact Matters

It is important to be "present" while you are in the same house. When you are living in close quarters with someone and not emotionally connected, you may feel lonelier than if you were alone. Maintaining eye contact with your partner is very important so that each of you feel seen and acknowledged.

Boundaries are Crucial

When you are spending almost all of your time in the same house or apartment, it is important to try to respect each other's space. If you are quarantined with young children, it is essential that you put them to bed early enough to have some "adult time." Even if you are just going on a walk together, couple's time is important.

Don't be "The Bickersons"

This is the time to let go of resentments and pettiness. Limiting the toxic energy of fighting is important for your physical, as well as your emotional, health.

Keep Your Sense of Humor

While our family was playing Monopoly, it struck my 21-year-old daughter as ridiculous how hard I was trying to make a deal with our 10-year-old, who stuck to his guns and refused. She laughed so hard that no sound came out and her eyes teared. I have carried that image with me for days. In a time when our future feels bleak and there is a sense of heaviness and fear around us, I am glad to have a moment of lightness and joy. Although it is easy to get caught up in the news and the dire situation, moments of levity and laughter are necessary to feed our souls.

Respect Each Other's Differences

Each person approaches moments of crisis in different ways. For example, one person may binge-watch news programs and read all he can about COVID-19, while the other person may want less information. My husband believes in reading everything he can about the crisis. I get overwhelmed by too much information.

Recently, when we were in bed, he was reading aloud about how COVID-19 was impacting NYC and I had to set a boundary. I told him that I would prefer to read my novel and did not want to hear more about the crisis before falling asleep so I would not have bad dreams or sleep fitfully.

Another difference that couples may experience in a crisis is that one person may be preoccupied with fears of taking risks while the other person wants to maintain a more normal life. Finally, after a disaster, one person in a couple may be more optimistic, proactive, and hopeful while the other is more passive, fatalistic, and pessimistic. It is not that one person is right and the other is wrong, it is simply that each person has a different style of coping with trauma.

Kind Gestures Go a Long Way

When my husband went to the grocery store to buy the essentials we needed, he added a pack of Twizzlers. We had been watching a lot of movies at home and he knows my favorite movie theater snack, so he bought it for me. Whether unloading the dish washer or massaging your partner's feet, caring gestures allow each person to feel valued. These are tough times and little acts of kindness can seem like luxuries that help us get through them.

Although there is no way to divorce-proof your marriage, especially not in a time of crisis like the coronavirus, being aware of the differences that you have and working hard to care for each other can help you move through almost any crisis with your relationships intact and potentially stronger. If you are not in a relationship, use this time to be kind to yourself and to focus on the positive qualities you have to offer. At the end of the day, COVID-19 may take away a lot of things, but it does not take away our ability to be loving to ourselves and others.

Also, I learned during this time that there is no perfect way to quarantine. Cohabitating is difficult, and it's important to use the conflicts and messy moments as opportunities to grow in your communication skills.

Kevin and Carol

It's really tough to be a cop during this time," my 37-year-old patient Kevin explained to me.

"Try to be a cop and a new mother. "It doubles your stress," his 28-year-old wife Carol replied.

Our first appointment was a Zoom call and even through a screen I could see the competitive dynamics between these two. They were referred to me from the Camden Police Department because they were a couple in danger of separating. Kevin and Carol had recently gotten married at City Hall after an unexpected pregnancy. Although they loved each other and both wanted the best outcome for their daughter Sophie, they certainly had a lot of life stressors to manage.

Similar to many of the police officers I have treated in the past year, they have had to cope with the chaos of their jobs along with the public's outcry in response to police brutality. After several horrific killings including George Floyd, an unarmed black man at the hands of a white police officer and Breonna Taylor, a young black woman who was fatally shot in her apartment after a forced entry by white police officers, there have been numerous protests against police brutality and racism. Working as a police officer in the city requires tolerating the judgment and shame from family members and other civilians as they challenge their decision to remain on the force. "I used to be proud of being a police officer," Carol said, "now I'm just ashamed and tired of being hated. I bring baby formula to my job and offer it to mothers with young babies but yesterday I was spit at."

Carol works day shifts while Kevin works nights in order to take turns watching Sophie. The problem with this arrangement is that they rarely spend any time together. Additionally, Kevin has been picking up shifts working a construction job in order to help pay their bills. They have recently started Sophie in daycare, but are afraid she may catch COVID-19. Both Carol and Kevin are sleep deprived and frequently snap at each other. When I asked Kevin what initially attracted him to Carol, he replied that he was drawn to her because "she was the most beautiful woman I've ever seen." He also loved the fact that she is more articulate than he is and is able to make conversation with anyone. When I asked Carol what she initially liked about Kevin she replied, "He is a good father to his 14-year-old son. He pays for his Catholic school and is very generous to his son's mother." Carol, a very practical, financially responsible woman, was impressed by Kevin's generosity and graciousness at first, but now it drives her crazy. She hates the fact that they are not more financially secure and that Kevin has never managed to save money. She is constantly criticizing him about his financial decisions, and he responds by withholding information about his debts, because he fears her anger.

Additionally, Carol's beauty, which initially attracted Kevin, has made him more insecure. He discovered that she had a relationship with another police officer before they got together and has barraged her with questions about the other man. He knows that the police department is a male-dominated environment and fears she will leave him as women have done in the past. Kevin grew up in "the poorest family in the poorest neighborhood in West Philadelphia." He has always had a strong work ethic and wanted to change his family's "lot in life." As a child, Kevin would get up early in the mornings before school and race to the local grocery store in order to get there before other local boys arrived in order to work bagging groceries for the day. Every penny he made was given to his mother as he attempted to earn her love. Unfortunately for Kevin, that never happened and his mother only seemed to care about the money he provided her. Both of Kevin's parents were neglectful and "more concerned about their own drinking and drug use than being parents." He no longer speaks to either of them.

Carol's parents split up after a tumultuous divorce and she was raised by her grandparents. The stability she received in her grandparents' home was a stark contrast to the conflict she witnessed between her parents. After watching her parents fight about money and infidelity issues, Carol vowed that she would do better for her family.

Because both Kevin and Carol had not had healthy models for communication, their conversations quickly deteriorated and they were frequently interrogating each other. Carol was looking to catch Kevin in a lie about his finances and Kevin was cross-examining Carol about her previous sexual experiences. Both were operating out of fear instead of expressing the love they had for each other in their hearts. After assessing the situation, I realized we needed to work quickly to build up this couple. I introduced the value of changing how they spoke to each other by adding compliments and decreasing criticisms. I also suggested altering the judgmental tone of their communication as well as slowing down the pace of what they were saying. Additionally, I recommended hiring a financial advisor to help them work out a plan on how to budget their money.

Lastly, we discussed how they could add some joy to their lives and not work all of the time. Kevin suggested going to the zoo with Sophie. In his childhood he had always wanted to go but his family had never had the money. They arranged to go as a family and had a great time. Although this couple still has a lot of work to do to improve their communication and be more supportive of each other, they are not willing to give up on their relationship. Each week they continue to show up for therapy in order to break their families' legacies of conflict and abandonment as well as cope with the stress of being police officers and new parents during a pandemic.

WHAT I HAVE LEARNED ABOUT MY PATIENTS DURING THIS TIME

When I went to include an example of a couple who was impacted during this time, I realized it was very difficult to select just one. We were all impacted by COVID-19. Some more than others, but no one got out unscathed. Some of us lost family members. Others got sick. Some lost jobs. Others lost businesses. Our children lost educational opportunities. We all became teachers, and nurses, and therapists. Many of us got sick of our spouses, our kids, and ourselves.

Those of us who fared well were master reframers. We learned to reframe our reality so we could discover the blessings during this time of loss. We became grateful for the little luxuries that we have. We learned to appreciate board games, puzzles, and delicious pizza shops that deliver. We learned to embrace hiking and we figured out how to celebrate family holidays through Zoom. We learned about our resilience.

In particular, my patients' resilience inspired me. They rarely canceled a session and quickly adapted to therapy through a computer screen.

I heard from patients whom I hadn't connected with in years. While struggling with losses, they remembered that therapy was a crucial tool that they could pull out of their tool kit and use in this time of crisis.

WHAT I HAVE LEARNED ABOUT MYSELF DURING THIS TIME

For the first time, I truly realized that therapists are essential workers. I felt honored to be a part of this group. What I further acknowledged about myself is that I am a person who shows up. From the moment the pandemic started, I felt needed by my patients. I knew I couldn't stop working, so I drove over to my office and figured out how to do Zoom and Facetime therapy. I worked ten-hour days in order to support my patients and tried to make sense of this unfathomable time. With the exception of a couple weeks in August, I just kept working. Even when my family got sick with COVID and we were all quarantining, I managed to do Zoom sessions from my bedroom. Although I was sick, others were sicker and more in need of support.

Over this past weekend I was driving and the famous U2 song, "One," came on the radio. As I was singing along with U2, I realized that I was getting the words wrong. There is a lyric that I thought said, "We **have** to carry each other," but instead I heard it incorrectly. What the lyrics actually say is, "We **get** to carry each other." That one word makes all the difference in the world. Instead of looking at it as a burden, the opportunity to take care of others is an incredible honor and a privilege. Whether it is taking care of patients, family members, or a romantic relationship, it is a gift that we all have the opportunity to be of service. I was grateful for the gift.

I also realized during this time that I could do with less material stuff. As someone who spent years engaging in "retail therapy" in order to soothe my own anxiety, I learned the value of living more simply. I don't want to imply that I'm completely cured, of course. I will never be a minimalist. But I have recognized the wasteful nature of the amount of shopping I used to do.

As an extroverted person, I also learned about the value of slowing down my social plans and giving myself time to write, meditate, and listen to my own inner dialogue. I spent less time on the phone and more time in front of my computer. I learned I could travel lighter. I only chose to see those people who truly made me happy, and I let go of some superfluous relationships.

I also learned, when the tennis courts reopened, that I could play tennis with a mask on and still run like the wind to get to the ball. I discovered that even if I lost a match, I would give it my all. I also realized that writing a book and sharing what I've learned gives me a sense of joy way deeper than anything I could buy. In this crazy, sad, soulful time of COVID, I discovered who I am at my core.

EXERCISE 1

What lessons have you learned during the time of COVID? Was it through your losses that you learned meaningful lessons, or was it through the act of quarantining that you gained a valuable piece of knowledge? List three things that you have learned during this time.

EXERCISE 2

How will you use these lessons to be a better employee, partner, or parent?

11

LIFE IS WHAT HAPPENS WHEN WE'RE BUSY MAKING OTHER PLANS

How do you handle your life when it throws you a curveball? What do you do when you or your partner confront an illness, lose a parent, or have a child with significant struggles? How do you cope with the discovery that there has been infidelity or dishonesty in your relationship? The challenge is to let go of "what should have been" so you can accept "what is." It's essential that you allow yourself the time to grieve the death of your vision.

GRIEVING

When someone close to us dies, it is often public knowledge. There is a funeral, a burial, and a time when friends and family step up to show support for the surviving family members. Friends bring meals, send condolence cards, and share memories about how loved the deceased person was. These losses are devastating. However, both the life of the deceased person and the survivors are acknowledged and honored through the sacred rituals of mourning.

Often, friends check in to see how the surviving family members are doing for months afterward. In the healthy grieving process, there is a sense of closure, as well as support. This grieving process has been widely discussed and understood both in literature and throughout popular culture.

However, there is another type of grief that is much more hidden and insidious. This is grief we experience when losses are significant yet not so easily defined. Dr. Pauline Boss coined the term "ambiguous loss" to explain the grief experienced from the loss of a loved one who is still alive but no longer physically or emotionally present, as occurs with addictions or the end of a relationship.

Dr. Boss initially wrote about this phenomenon to describe the grief that occurs when there is the trauma of a missing child or a loved one who is away from home serving his or her country. I believe it can be expanded to describe situations related to addiction, infidelity, and other forms of intimate betrayal. Sexual betrayal, for example, is devastating and can lead to separation or divorce, and the "death of the dream of an intact family." If there is an emotional or financial betrayal, that can lead to feeling scared and not safe. And addictions of all types create devastating physical and emotional absences, even though the family member may still be alive and physically present.

We can also suffer ambiguous grief when a loved one experiences a significant illness and is not functioning in his or her former state. For example, tremendous grief occurs for the whole family when a parent experiences Alzheimer's and is no longer living like his or her vibrant self. Additionally, grief occurs when a child is diagnosed with a learning disability or a significant health condition. Often, we experience the death of the dream of our expectations for that child. Another example is the grief we carry when a close family member or friend experiences cancer.

Sometimes, layers of ambiguous grief build up. You feel intense grief but you are not sharing it publicly because the elements of your grief seem trivial or shameful, or because you're honoring your loved one's wishes for privacy. However, that ambiguous grief is frozen inside you. If you're like many clients I've treated over the years, you may believe you do not have the right to feel sad. You might also think you need to be strong for your family members.

When frozen grief is released, it turns into shame and a general sense of feeling deficient. Worse still, it can be somaticized and felt deeply in your body as aches and pains, or a sense of heaviness. Sometimes it can lead to depression, anxiety, or a feeling of not wanting to get out of bed in the morning. Frozen grief manifests itself differently in everyone, but one thing is for sure, no one gets out of life unscathed or avoids grief.

KÜBLER-ROSS'S 5 STAGES OF GRIEF

In 1969, Elizabeth Kübler-Ross described five common stages of grief: denial, anger, bargaining, depression, and acceptance. These stages describe responses to grief that most people have. However, there is not a typical response to grief because loss impacts all of us in different ways. The five stages provide a framework that helps us make sense of the process of grieving, but the stages are not linear and some people may not experience all of them.

The first stage of grief is denial, and this is what initially helps us to survive the loss. In this stage, we are not living in actual reality; instead, we are living in "preferable" reality. Shock and denial lead us to feel numb. This is nature's way of letting in only as much grief as we can handle. Instead of us being completely overwhelmed by our feelings, we stay in a state of shock and denial.

The second stage of grief is anger. This is a necessary stage of the healing process, even though it may feel overwhelming and endless. The more we truly feel our anger, the more quickly it will dissipate and the more we will heal. This anger may extend to our family members, friends, ourselves, and even God. We may blame ourselves for our mistakes or rage at God for not protecting us from devastating losses. Underneath all of that anger is pain.

The third stage is bargaining. This is a time of negotiation when we find ourselves making deals with God. "Please God, if you heal my husband, I will be the best wife and never complain again." "If I spend my life volunteering and helping others, can this time just be a bad dream?" We become lost in a world of "What if…" and "If only…" statements. Guilt often accompanies the bargaining stage, as we think of what we could have done differently.

The fourth stage, depression, brings us to the reality of the present situation. We feel the emptiness as grief enters our lives in a deeper way. It is important to mention that this depression is not a sign of mental illness but an appropriate response to a great loss. At this stage, we often withdraw from life and stay stuck in a fog of intense sadness.

The fifth stage is acceptance. People often confuse this stage with the notion of being OK with what happened. That may never be the case. We may never like this new reality, but eventually we will accept it. It will become the new norm with which we have to live. In this stage, we begin to invest in our friendships and relationships with ourselves as we accept our new reality.

HOW CAN YOU GRIEVE EFFECTIVELY?

The first step in processing grief is acknowledging that you are experiencing a significant loss, whether it is easily apparent, such as the loss of a loved one, or more hidden, such as an infidelity in your marriage or a child's addiction. Your perfect vision for your life has been shattered and it takes time to heal your heart. This is the time for journaling, meditation, and looking within yourself in order to help you experience the myriad of feelings that are occurring and giving yourself permission to experience any of Kübler- Ross's stages, including denial, anger, bargaining, depression, and the overwhelming pain that occurs as you try to accept your loss.

It is important that you not rush the grief process by pushing yourself to "get over it" quickly. The act of writing letters to the person who has hurt you is valuable, along with writing letters to God. Extreme self-care is also valuable at this time, including exercise, eating well, resting, and limiting activities that do not bring you joy.

ACCEPTING THAT YOU ARE IN HOLLAND, NOT PARIS

Years ago, I had a patient who had an autistic son. This devoted mother explained to me that she adored her son, but he was not who she and her husband were expecting when they first got pregnant. She shared with me an analogy that she used to describe her situation. She explained that when she and her husband were planning to have a baby, she viewed it as similar to planning a trip to Paris. "When you are planning a trip to Paris, you anticipate the journey. You shop for it. You imagine the people that you will meet, the sights you will see, and the foods that you will taste. You prepare by buying travel guides, learning about the language and the culture. Then, somehow, you realize that your trip was rerouted and you end up in Holland. It is not that Holland isn't great. It just isn't Paris." She clarified that her having an autistic child was like going to Holland when she expected Paris. She further explained, "Holland is a scenic place to visit with interesting people and lessons to be learned, but it is just not the journey that I expected."

After their son was first diagnosed, my patient and her husband learned extensively about autism, took advantage of all the resources that were offered to them, and met some incredible people along the way. However, at times, she deeply grieved that she never had the opportunity to experience Paris.

So much of life reminds me of this insightful patient's analogy. We have expectations that often do not get met. Part of our journey on this planet is about letting go of what should be and accepting what is. Whether it is accepting that you have a special needs child, or a partner with an addiction, or an imperfect marriage, life reroutes us all the time. For many people, it is getting a divorce or losing a loved one that catapults them into this other culture that they never thought they would be in. The challenge for all of us is to hold our heads high and stay present for the adventure, even though it is one we never pictured ourselves experiencing.

OPTION B

In life, so much of our struggle is about letting go of how we think things should be so we can accept how they actually are. Sheryl Sandberg, Chief Operating Officer of Facebook, described this phenomenon eloquently two weeks after her husband died unexpectedly. Sheryl realized that there was a Father-Daughter dance on the schedule and she no longer had a husband who could take their daughter. "I want Dave," she cried out to her friend, after he offered to escort her daughter.

Her friend empathetically understood her grief, but then he took a deep breath and said, "Option A is not available. So, let's kick the shit out of Option B." And so, this loving friend escorted Sheryl's daughter to the dance and made sure she did not feel left out. The best part was that he and Sheryl's daughter actually had a good time. Although no one was under the illusion that he was a replacement for the young girl's father, it didn't take away from allowing her to experience a great night with her friends.

After there are heartbreaks, whether those heartbreaks are through death, divorce, disappointment, or other losses, there is an ending to Option A. Resiliency occurs when we dust ourselves off and adjust to Option B. We accept the reality that no one's life works out perfectly the way he or she wants it to. However, we will still experience beauty, joy, and value—once we accept Option B.

Sue

When Sue married Matt, she thought her fairy tale had finally come true. She felt like she deserved it, too. She was the only one in her blue-collar family who had graduated from college, and had spent her twenties working two jobs in order to put herself through graduate school at night. And even with that, she had spent years working extra-hard to pay off her college and graduate school loans.

Unlike her two sisters who had gotten pregnant while in high school, Sue was the high-achieving sibling. She had little time for dating, as she spent all of her energy completing her master's degree in speech pathology. Her two best friends from her graduate school program, Amy and Sean, had finally done a "dating intervention." They set up a Match.com profile and begged Sue to begin online dating.

In a very short time, Sue met Matt. Matt was the antithesis of Sue, who was serious and hard-working. He was lighthearted and curious about everything. He was very intelligent and had a lot of information about many different topics, but hadn't committed to any one area of study or expertise.

Shortly after meeting, Matt shared with Sue that he had

almost ten years in recovery from prescription pills and cocaine. He explained to Sue that his drug use was in the past and he now was grateful to have a new perspective on life. He told her that he loved children and dreamed of becoming an elementary school teacher. Sue knew about working hard and making dreams become reality, and pictured Matt doing exactly that.

Sue and Matt initially became friends, and Sue encouraged Matt to go back to college and begin working on his education degree. As Matt began taking his first college classes, the two of them realized that they had romantic feelings for each other and started dating. After a short courtship, they decided to get married and then quickly got pregnant.

At this point, Matt decided to stop taking classes because formal education was not really his thing. Instead, he decided to stay home with their baby during the day and drive for Uber in the evenings to supplement Sue's salary from her speech therapy job. This seemed logical to them, as Sue was the larger wage earner. While Sue worked at the hospital, Matt would send her videos of their daughter, Ivy, on the playground or on a nature walk through out the neighborhood. He seemed to be doing an excellent job as Ivy's caretaker.

Matt was a natural-born teacher and would constantly talk to Ivy throughout the day, teaching her vocabulary words and reading her books. Sue had never been happier. Until she got the phone call at work from her mother-in-law. Her mother-in-law had come over for lunch and was supposed to stay and watch Ivy, so that Matt could pick up an extra Uber shift. When she got there, Ivy was crying in her crib while Matt was on the floor in the bathroom. He had overdosed from using cocaine and died.

Sue was completely shocked. She had no knowledge that he

had been using drugs at all in their marriage and could not make any sense of this information. It did not fit with the Matt she knew.

When Sue first came in for therapy, it was just three weeks after Matt died. The shock was still evident on her face as she said, "I'm only 37 years old and I'm a widow. How am I supposed to take care of my 18-month-old daughter? Ivy spent every single day of her life with her dad. What am I supposed to do now?" We both took a moment and just breathed together. This was one of those times where I was so glad that I could borrow my favorite 12-step slogan, and I told her that she could just take it "one day at a time."

Our first order of business was taking care of the practical aspects of her life, and we filled out her disability forms together after she decided that she needed some time away from work to figure out a plan. Our second order of business was Ivy. Sue did not have the luxury of breaking down in her grief. She had an 18-month-old to take care of. Ivy had never gone to a babysitter or a daycare center. However, Sue was now a single working mother and would need help. Because Sue was incredibly independent and prideful, she was not used to accepting help from others. We spoke about needing to change this part of herself and working on accepting love and support from friends and extended family. Her homework assignment was to accept the meals her friends were sending over graciously, and to ask Amy and Sean about the daycare center where they sent their three children.

Sue's immediate family was not very helpful. Her nurturing mother had died several years previously, and her father was never very involved in her life. Her two sisters meant well but were overwhelmed by the needs of their own children, as they were both single mothers struggling financially.

Surprisingly, Sue found love and support in places that she had never even realized that she had. Her father's brother stepped up and offered to babysit for her every week when she came to therapy. He was an auto mechanic who had never had children of his own. He decided to make Sue his "honorary daughter" and Ivy his "honorary granddaughter." Her mother's mother also offered to watch the baby and cook for them. Additionally, Matt's family was very supportive. Her father-in-law came over to help her go through the financial papers. Together they realized that Matt's drug use had been going on for months and he had used up their savings on his cocaine habit.

Sue's friends became her "angel network." When Sue realized that Matt had not been paying the mortgage and their house was going to be foreclosed, Amy and Sean insisted that she and Ivy move in with them. Ivy started at the same daycare center that their children went to and would come home and they would all eat meals together, after the three adults would return from work. Suddenly, Ivy was being raised with "siblings" and was thriving. And Sue's best friend Bobby called to check in on her every single night, making sure she remembered how to laugh.

In therapy, Sue began to address some of her grief. She had been blindsided by Matt's overdose and had to work hard to get through her feelings of sadness and betrayal. As hurt as she was by his behavior, she also acknowledged that he had been an amazing father to Ivy during the first year and a half of her life. It was difficult to come to terms with the fact that he had so many wonderful qualities, yet he had been getting high around their daughter. She began to look at herself and how she had been working so intensely between her job and taking care of Ivy that she had missed what was going on right in front of her.

Part of our therapy included recognizing that two truths could occur at the same time. Sue's husband did love her and his daughter, but he was also relapsing. Sue realized that she could be sad and grieving but at the same time feel blessed and grateful. She was a spiritual woman and believed that her mother and Matt had reconnected and were watching over her and Ivy. Sue explained, "They are two more angels in my angel network who want good things to happen to us."

Her mother had been a beautiful supportive presence to Sue while she was growing up and had introduced her to a love of nature—in particular dragonflies. Matt had only known her mother for a year before she died but had coincidentally shared with her his appreciation of dragonflies, and the two of them had compared photographs of this insect. After a year of counseling, Sue described a recent afternoon when she was outside with Amy and Sean drinking a glass of lemonade while watching all four kids play in the backyard swimming pool. Two colorful dragonflies landed right next to her foot. Sue believed that they were a sign from her mother and Matt that everything was going to be alright.

GRIEVING THE LOSS OF A DREAM

As I mentioned previously in this chapter, you don't have to lose a loved one to experience grief. Sometimes there is simply the loss of a dream. Unlike Sue in the previous example, who grieved the loss of her husband, Stacey initially grieved the loss of her vision for her life. Stacey had always imagined herself falling in love, getting married, and then becoming a mother. When life didn't work out like she planned, she began to change her perspective and adjust to Option B. Stacey was a 38-year-old woman who had made the difficult decision to do whatever it took to become a mother.

When she called to set up our first session, she had lots of questions. "What are your views on in vitro fertilization? Have you ever counseled anyone who was considering using a sperm donor? Do you think it's possible to be a good mom without a partner?" After "vetting" me on the phone, Stacey determined that I could be a supportive therapist during this overwhelming time.

Stacey worked full-time as a veterinarian after putting herself through the grueling process of vet school. During her twenties and thirties, she had lived through a series of unhealthy relationships with men who did not treat her well. Her last relationship was the most toxic and she believed this man had few redeeming qualities. The only reason that Stacey had endured this emotionally abusive relationship was because she wanted to have a partner with whom to have a baby. It had finally dawned on her that this man would make a terrible father. After breaking up with him, she had a realization that she could become a mother on her own.

Stacey was adopted herself, and wanted to have another person on this planet with her own genes. She had been reading up on in vitro fertilization and had realized that she wanted to get off of her anxiety medication in order to have a healthy pregnancy. She was also aware that she would need the support of a therapist to help her navigate the whole process. She asked me if I would be in for the long haul. I reassured her that her values aligned with my own and I would happily be on board.

Her adoptive parents lived out of state and she did not believe they would provide much emotional support due to their religious beliefs as well as their own anxiety. Over the next year, she found a sperm donor and went through three cycles of invitrofertilization until it finally resulted in a pregnancy. After each cycle did not work, Stacey grieved the loss and experienced anger at her own body for letting her down. The financial cost was also exorbitant, and she realized that she was running out of money. Additionally, she grieved the reality that she was going through this whole process without a partner. This was not the future she had envisioned for herself. She grieved the "white picket fence" image that was not coming to fruition.

When Stacey finally managed to become pregnant, she was "cautiously optimistic." She was afraid to get too excited because she was "waiting for the other shoe to drop." Each week when she came to therapy, she would let me know how big her fetus was getting. It went from the size of a pea to the size of a lemon while still remaining healthy. Without her anxiety medication, Stacey was filled with worries. What if she lost the baby? What if the baby was not healthy? How was she going to handle being a single working mother? Could she really do this on her own? To soothe her anxiety, we worked on developing coping skills including: building a healthy support network and incorporating more self-care into her life.

We discovered a local support group called Single Parents By Choice. This group was a game changer for Stacey. The women in the group were incredibly reassuring and positive. They provided her role models of how to successfully handle being a single parent. They were very inclusive and began inviting her to their weekly get togethers while she was still pregnant. More than just being role models to one another, they were each other's lifelines. They provided her with recommendations for a daycare center, pediatrician, and local babysitters. The women in the support group shared their stories as well as suggestions on how to cope after giving birth. These women quickly became the sisters she never had, and after she gave birth to a healthy baby boy, they sent her meals for a week and also came over to clean her apartment.

During Stacey's time in therapy, we revised her vision of what family is. Also, we worked on clarifying what she could ask for from her adoptive parents. Despite some of their limitations, they loved her and wanted to get to know their grandchild. We developed some healthy boundaries to help them maintain their role in her life.

After having her baby, Stacey experienced a love deeper than any she had ever imagined. At the beginning of each therapy session, she would show me the latest pictures she had taken of her son on her phone. The women in her support group continued to be her tribe, along with a trusted babysitter and a reliable pediatrician. Her world had gone from "black and white" to "multicolored" as it became filled with beautiful relationships. Although it was not the traditional future she had pictured, it was a full, rich life bursting with love and joy.

EXERCISE 1

Write a letter to the person who hurt you. If there is not an identifiable person, write a letter to God. The purpose for writing this letter is not to share it with the person who harmed you. Instead, it is a way of venting your feelings of pain, anger, and sadness.

EXERCISE 2

When your Option A did not work out the way you originally imagined, how were you able to successfully adjust to Option B? If you have not yet done that, allow yourself the space to picture what adjusting to Option B will look like. Journal about it.

EXERCISE 3

Do you believe in spiritual signs? If so, have any occurred in your life? Write them down, as well as what you believe was the meaning behind their presence.

12

THE LOVE YOU TAKE
IS EQUAL TO
THE LOVE YOU MAKE

NO PARTNER WILL MEET
ALL YOUR NEEDS

Here is something you already know: your partner will not meet all your needs. Maintaining a healthy support system, including family members, friends, mentors, sponsors, and a therapist is crucial to a multifaceted lifelong partnership. It is also important to practice your own self-care, including exercise, hobbies, support groups, and therapy.

Maintaining friendships enriches our lives. But even more important you must truly become your own best friend. And, yes, I know it sounds like a cliché. I have had many patients bristle when they hear me say it. What becoming your own best friend means, however, is that you must treat yourself with kindness and compassion.

Go back to the exercise in chapter one with the picture of yourself as a small child. Look at that picture. Do not allow yourself to berate that child. That wounded child did the best he or she could to cope with many difficult situations. It is essential that you stop emotionally abusing that child by speaking to him or her in a judgmental or critical tone. Allow that child (who still lives within you) to take breaks from work, to rest, and to eat well.

Recognize that your partner is a wounded child, too. When you start talking in a kinder voice to yourself, you will begin speaking in a more compassionate voice to your partner, also. Remember the Karpman Drama Triangle where you viewed yourself as a as a victim, perpetrator, or rescuer? It is important to end those roles. When you look at both yourself and your partner as injured children who are doing your best, you will be better able to show honesty and vulnerability in front of each other. You will also learn to give openheartedly and you will be able to receive love back. Some of that love may come from your partner, but much of it will come from your support network.

NO ONE DOES LIFE PERFECTLY. WHY SHOULD YOUR RELATIONSHIP BE ANY DIFFERENT?

It is OK to make mistakes, to struggle in our communication and to hurt each other's feelings. The important part is owning our mistakes, being authentic and vulnerable, and trying to do better next time. One of my favorite quotes is from the movie Scent of a Woman. Al Pacino says, "When you get tangled up, tango on." What he means is that we must recalibrate our navigation system by doing the next right thing.

Sometimes that is not easy to do. When we grow up in families where we are expected to be perfect, owning our mistakes and being accountable is difficult. However, becoming accountable get easier with practice. It is essential that we give ourselves, as well as our partner and other loved ones, the opportunity to make mistakes, and that we practice forgiving ourselves and each other.

THE HEART OF THE MATTER

Don Henley's song, "The Heart of the Matter," soulfully describes the process of forgiveness. He explains how people come and go in our lives and at times deeply disappoint us, but if we carry that anger it will eat us up inside. Don Henley sums up the heart of the matter as simply being about forgiveness, even if the love is no longer there.

For so many of my patients and even myself, the anger and righteous rage that Don Henley describes keeps us stuck in victim mode. When we are victims, it is easy to justify the negative behaviors of victimizing ourselves and others. We may turn that hurt onto ourselves by over-eating or disappearing through drug and alcohol use. We may express the hurt directly to our partners in a rageful manner or through passive aggressive behaviors with the intent to wound. It is also easy to take out our frustrations on another family member by overreacting to his or her behaviors.

It is crucial to work through our feelings so we can stop hurting ourselves and others, and so eventually we can heal. Underneath the anger is often sadness and disappointment. We can't outrun it. Once we grieve the losses, we will be free to move on and be in alignment with our true selves.

In a Peloton cycling class I take, the instructor, Robin Arzon, says, "Through our pain is our power." Instead of hiding from our pain, it is important that we embrace it. No one gets out of life or relationships without experiencing pain. Once we acknowledge those deep losses and grieve them, we can change into a softer, kinder version of ourselves. We learn humility as well as acceptance. We keep walking forward.

HOW DO YOU WALK FORWARD?

Realize Every Relationship is Like a Ferris Wheel

There are highs and lows on a Ferris wheel, as each couple enters their own little carriage. Sometimes the heights are scary and it might feel easier to get off the ride. However, if you get off the ride too early you will miss the breathtaking view from the top.

It is unrealistic, however, to believe that your ride will stay at the top forever. The bottom of the ride allows you to anticipate getting up higher. The climb up is the hard work involved in building to the pinnacle. When we expect perfection in our relationships, we imagine staying at the top forever, but there is no adventure in that.

Change Your Self Talk and the Way You Talk to Others

Instead of berating your partner or yourself for your less-than-ideal moments, or those instances when you are at the bottom of the Ferris wheel, show compassion. We are all just "Bozos on the bus," doing the best we can.

Compassion for yourself and your partner can go a long way. This could look like talking to both yourself and others more gently and less critically, recognizing that we all have wounded children inside us. This does not mean accepting bad behaviors. It means speaking up for your wounded child within when you feel "triggered" by another person's behaviors. It also means being accountable and admitting when your behavior has injured someone else.

Develop Rituals

One way that we can begin to repair our relationships is to create sacred habits or rituals that ground us. We can practice rituals alone, with a partner, or with our whole families. A daily ritual can be something simple, such as sharing a few cups of coffee or tea in the morning and talking about our intentions for the day. Rituals can involve exercise, such as a walk around the neighborhood together in the evening to discuss the events that occurred during the time apart. Rituals can involve praying together, practicing a morning meditation together, or writing in a journal. A ritual could involve a loving gesture, such as a goodbye kiss before you leave for the office. Some full-family rituals might include saying grace before you eat dinner together or having the same relatives over every year for your holiday celebrations.

RITUALS I PRACTICE TO BE PRESENT FOR MY PATIENTS AND TAKE CARE OF MYSELF

Before I see patients in my office, I have several rituals that ground me. I make a delicious cup of gourmet coffee, light a candle, and take a quiet moment to breathe. As I exhale, I focus on being my best self in order to help my patients heal. My intentions are pure and my hope is enormous.

I also keep a vase filled with fresh flowers to remind myself of all of the beauty in the world. I take in their glorious colors, the aroma that accompanies them and feel soothed no matter what trauma I end up hearing about from my patients. My love of flowers also connects me to my relationship with my grandmother. She was an avid gardener and took me to the Philadelphia Flower Show several times before she died. When I see the flowers sitting on my table, it reminds me of the power of family and service. My paternal grandmother was a social worker who spent her career working for the Philadelphia School System. My mother was also a healer. Through her work as an inner-city guidance counselor, she helped hundreds of students and families. Gazing at these flowers reminds me of the legacy I come from and the job I am supposed to do on this planet. The simple acts of engaging my sense of taste, smell, and sight bring me to the present moment.

My rituals also help me to slow down and separate from my own home life. When I practice them in my office, I leave my everyday worries behind and focus on the important work of being of service to my patients.

After my day at work, I listen to music on the way home in order to leave my work life behind. The act of listening to music engages the sense of sound and helps me leave my patients' concerns behind. After I get home, I change out of my work attire into soft and comfortable clothing that engages my sense of touch and helps me transition back into my roles as a wife and mother. These decompression rituals keep me from taking home the vicarious trauma of my patients, thereby allowing me to be present in my own life.

Another name for these decompression rituals is grounding techniques. Grounding techniques are strategies that help a person mange traumatic memories or strong emotions by distancing them from their feelings by using their five senses to bring them back into the present. These grounding techniques help me let go of the traumatic stories and pain I am holding for my patients.

HEALER, HEAL THYSELF

When we don't take care of ourselves as healers, we are susceptible to developing addictions, depression, or anxiety. The following story shows what happened to an accomplished oncologist, George, when he did not set rituals or follow boundaries in his life.

George

George was a brilliant pediatric oncologist. He worked over 90 hours a week trying to help children and their families heal from cancer. He had been married for almost 35 years to his high school sweetheart, Tracy. George was a very charismatic and charming man with a big heart. To blow off steam from his intense work week, George had spent the last decade performing as the lead singer and guitarist in a local band with other physicians.

George frequently traveled to other cities in order to present at medical conferences about the groundbreaking work he was doing. In the field, George was treated as a "rock star physician." The fact that he actually played rock music with his band was a bonus. However, George had many secrets. He was leading a double life and had an Adderall and cocaine addiction. He was also engaging in multiple ongoing affairs.

George was referred to me by the Pennsylvania Physician's Health Program (PHP) after his multiple affairs with nurses and other office staff were discovered in the hospital. One of the nursing assistants filed a complaint with human resources, a thorough investigation began, and his house of cards came tumbling down. On his work computer, hospital administrators discovered pornography and naked pictures women had been sending to him. Additionally, there were complaints from other physicians that he was coming to work high on drugs, and a toxicology report showed that both Adderall and cocaine were in his system.

In our work together, we discovered that George had both a drug addiction and a sex and love addiction. For years, he had compartmentalized his life and managed to be an attentive husband and father of two children while hiding his ongoing affairs and drug use. Tracy was shocked as their perfect world was shattered. I referred her to a colleague so that she could have her own safe person with whom to process the tremendous trauma of the betrayal.

This was George's first experience with therapy, and he questioned the need to discuss any painful parts of his history. "My childhood was just fine," he initially said. "It was a lot better than it could have been." George shared that at the age of one he had been adopted by a kind older German couple and was raised as an only child. His biological mother was an addict who had him out of wedlock when she was just a teenager. He did not know who his biological father was but had fantasies that he was both brilliant and talented.

The couple who adopted George were quiet and studious. They were happy to have a child, but did not have much energy or warmth to lavish on him. They taught him about the value of hard work through academic achievement, and George learned how to please them by succeeding in an academic capacity.

Nevertheless, George felt very different than his parents and at times was suffocated by the sterile environment. During his childhood he spent many hours fantasizing that he would be rescued by his birth parents and they would adore him. As a junior in high school, he started dating Tracy, who was a sophomore. She adored him and felt lucky to have a handsome and talented upperclassman show interest in her. What she did not have knowledge of was the fact that he was having sex with other young women while they were dating.

Tracy came from a large Italian family that embraced George as one of their own. He loved the sense of belonging that her loud and boisterous family provided him. Throughout college and medical school, he continued to be in a relationship with Tracy while secretly dating other women.

George and Tracy got married after his first year in medical school, and Tracy worked as an accountant to help pay for his education. In their twenties, George's career trajectory took off and he became a rising star in the medical community. Tracy moved with him to both Boston and Texas as various prestigious children's hospitals recruited him.

By the time George and Tracy were in their early thirties, they had two children: a boy and a girl. Their perfect family was complete. Tracy stayed home to raise their children but felt isolated, being far away from her tightly knit family. George began traveling to medical conferences where he was revered as an innovator in the field. His research on curing childhood cancer was brilliant and his charismatic way of communicating information made him a sought-after lecturer on the workshop circuit.

When George would travel to other cities, he would have one-night stands with women in the medical community. Until he met Gloria. Gloria was also a married doctor who presented at conferences. After they began an affair, she introduced George to cocaine. Their relationship was intense and exciting and they continued to meet in various cities, intensifying their risk-taking by using drugs and drinking excessive amounts of alcohol together.

When George returned to the hospital after these binges, he continued to use stimulants to cope with the many demands he faced. He found that both Adderall and cocaine kept him energized and able to cope with all of the crises that he needed to solve in a day. He enjoyed the adoration he received from both his patient's families and staff alike. His flirtations and risk-taking at the hospital increased. Unfortunately, there was not enough adoration and acceptance in the world to soothe his underlying feeling that he was a fraud. He still pictured himself as that baby who was given away, not loved enough to be kept.

When George came to see me, he was shellshocked. His reputation at the hospital had been destroyed and he was in danger of being fired. He was also worried about losing his medical license, which was a huge part of his identity. Additionally, he feared losing his marriage and his relationship with his children as well as his whole extended family. He was devastated and had thoughts of ending his life. My first order of business with him was to provide him with hope, as well as educate him about addictions. I wanted to be honest about the tremendous amount of work he had ahead of him, but I also wanted to convey a sense of optimism that I believed his life could turn around.

He was an avid reader and read every book I recommended including *The Wounded Healer* by Richard Irons and Jennifer Schneider. He also willingly went to all of the 12-step groups that I suggested, including Sex and Love Addicts Anonymous (SLAA), Alcoholics Anonymous (AA), and Caduceus Groups (a support system for medical professionals who have the desire to recover from chemical addictions using a 12-step approach). Additionally, he joined an addictions therapy group in my practice where he addressed boundary issues and made connections with other recovering men.

It was necessary for George to let go of many unhealthy behaviors, including communication with all of his acting out partners. He needed to get rid of his cell phone and get a new phone number. He committed to ending all friendships with women where there was any flirtation or sexual innuendo. He also gave up all drug and alcohol use, including caffeine because he was drinking five or more cups of coffee every day.

The Physician's Health Program was a tremendous help for George as well, and he agreed to have them monitor him for the next several years by providing urine screens and allowing them to consult with me as his treating psychologist. We worked on increasing his integrity through practicing honesty in his relationships and setting boundaries in both his work and personal life. We also began to explore his relationship with God and how he had let go of his belief in a higher power early on in his career after watching too many of his young patients die.

For the first time in his marriage, George was completely honest with his wife about his behaviors. Although she experienced a tremendous amount of pain, she did not leave him. He was truly shocked that someone could know his dark side and still stand by him. As an adopted child, he was convinced that if anyone knew his worst behaviors, that person would abandon him just like his biological mother did. This was not the case.

Despite all of the work George did on himself, he was still let go by the prestigious hospital where he was employed. That was one of the consequences of his behavior. He took the job termination hard and grieved the loss of his identity as a "superstar doctor." I continued to counsel him regularly while he was unemployed and had to figure out who he was without the label of being a doctor.

Concurrently, he and his wife worked on building a more honest and genuine relationship. After several years, he was offered a new job in a hospital in the Midwest. This time he went into the opportunity honestly, speaking up in his interview about a work-life balance and only being able to work

40 hours a week without traveling to conferences. He shared with the interviewing doctors that he was in recovery and needed to continue to attend 12-step meetings and therapy. The interviewers respected his honesty and gave him a chance.

As we prepared to end our therapy together, I let him know how impressed I was with his transparency and his ability to advocate for himself. I happily referred him to a colleague who lived in the city where he was relocating. For many years after I treated him, I would receive an annual holiday card where he expressed his gratitude for my belief in him.

Both George and Tracy are still committed to their relationship, and George continues to work his program of recovery. They have changed many aspects of their lives. George now works shorter days and begins each morning with a walk around the neighborhood with Tracy where they discuss their intentions for the day. After an eight-hour shift at the hospital, he attends a 12-step support group. Tracy also attends a weekly partners of addicts therapy group and discusses her own fears and concerns with George. They are consciously aware of the fragility of their relationship and do their best to nurture it consistently.

NOT ALL RELATIONSHIPS ARE MEANT TO LAST

Although one of the premises of this book is that it is important to realize there is no such thing as a perfect relationship, not all relationships should be endured. When only one person in a relationship is committed to trying to salvage it, it may be necessary to walk away. Sometimes it is healthier for a person to leave a dysfunctional relationship in order to stay in his or her own integrity.

Faith

Faith was a minister's daughter who was a former Homecoming Queen. At 33 years old she was still beautiful with a sparkling smile and long blond hair. Along with being the Homecoming Queen, she had been her high school's valedictorian and a varsity volleyball player. She was a member of dozens of high school clubs and had prided herself on being friends with every group of students in her senior class. On top of all of her school activities, she had volunteered in church, prepared food for the area soup kitchens, and sung with her church choir at local hospitals and prisons. Faith had grown up in a family that taught her to stay busy, be selfless in her giving, and always strive to do her best. Faith was raised to be perfect.

Faith earned a full scholarship to a local college where she was on the Dean's list earning stellar grades in her marketing major. She worked full time in a small grocery store on campus and managed to juggle both her academics and her full-time job seamlessly. In every single area of her life, Faith was soaring. Except in her choice of men. Faith consistently chose men who were beneath her. They weren't ambitious, driven, or hardworking. Also, they weren't respectful of her or particularly kind. After having a one-night stand with a young man she met at a fraternity party, Faith found herself pregnant and alone. Suddenly, her life plan went off course.

Fortunately, Faith's family's Christian values helped them to accept her pregnancy and support her as she had the baby and still managed to graduate from college with honors. After graduation, she quickly got a job marketing for a national cereal company, where she moved up the company ladder with record speed. She became indispensable in the workplace and often managed to work longer and harder than anyone else in the company. When her daughter's daycare was closed, Faith would bring her along to the office. She even bought her daughter a toy briefcase. She would joke that both she and her daughter were "working girls."

During this time, Faith reconnected with a man she had known from high school. He still lived locally and had not gone to college. He was working as an auto mechanic and took both Faith and her daughter out to dinner. After a very brief courtship, they decided to get married and quickly had two more babies. Before long, Faith had three young children under seven years old.

At this time, Faith's career trajectory was skyrocketing. She led a team of over 50 employees. Her coworkers gave her nicknames like "Superwoman" and "The Energizer Bunny." Whenever there was an opportunity to lead a committee or take on a new project, Faith happily volunteered. No one knew how she did it. She always had a smile on her face, even when she worked 80 hours a week.

At home, Faith managed to cook nutritious meals, keep a clean house, and drop her babies off at daycare. The more she did, the less her husband had to do. Eventually, he stopped doing even the minimal chores of taking out the garbage or chopping wood for the fireplace. The less he did, the more she compensated.

The problem was Faith was exhausted. Her husband did not respect all of the work that she was doing and would frequently make disparaging comments, putting her down or insulting women in general. He had several affairs and counted on her forgiving nature to let him off the hook. Looking at the inequality in her marriage was too painful for Faith, so instead she buried herself in work and received her positive recognition and appreciation from the workplace.

Therapy was difficult for Faith to put into her schedule because of her workaholic lifestyle. Whenever a career opportunity came up, it was difficult for her to say no. Because she spent so much time in the car driving for work and was such a good student, I gave her audiobook recommendations that she could listen to in her car including *The Drama of The Gifted Child* by Alice Miller and *Codependent No More* by Melody Beatty. I started to plant seeds that maybe she deserved more in her life than the way she had been living. Instead of addressing the unhappiness that she was experiencing in her marriage directly, we decided to focus on her.

Many years ago, when I was in graduate school, I had a professor who said that "activity is an antidote for anxiety." I shared this quote with Faith. Because Faith was constantly busy, she rarely had a chance to feel her feelings. The dissatisfaction in her marriage, as well as her depression and anxiety, became numb as she focused all of her energy on her career. The famous recovery author John Bradshaw said it best, "We are human beings not human doings." One of our goals in working together was to get Faith to slow down and realize what she was feeling, as well as what she wanted out of her life.

In therapy, Faith confided to me that although her company provided her with three weeks of paid time off a year, she had not taken a single day. So, we started with baby steps. Faith's homework was to take better care of herself by taking a half day off on a Friday. The goal was to not fill the time cleaning her house, preparing food for her family, or volunteering to take care of anyone in the community. Faith admitted that she did not know what she would do. Relaxation was a concept that she was not allowed as a child, and it initially felt selfish and indulgent for her.

Although Faith had splurged on a Peloton bike, she had never even set it up, believing that exercise was a luxury for other people, not herself. Additionally, she admitted that she viewed herself as a terrible friend because she never made time to see her girlfriends. We decided that her first Friday afternoon off would include a hike with her girlfriend, whom she had not seen in months. This friend was someone whom Faith viewed as extremely brave because she had left an abusive marriage and was now living independently. Faith told me that every time she spoke to her friend, she felt inspired. She also acknowledged that hiking outside and noticing the fall leaves changing colors would be "good for her soul." She promised me that she would take that afternoon for herself simply to pursue joy.

In 12-step recovery rooms there is a slogan, "Bring the body and the mind will follow." What that means is that instead of waiting until you are properly motivated to change before taking action, just take action and the act of doing the behavior will be reinforcing enough to modify your thinking. For Faith, the act of being accountable to me in therapy encouraged her to treat herself better. Additionally, she began to look at some of the perfectionistic messages that she had held on to since childhood. She realized how much pressure was put on her since she was a young girl and acknowledged how her mother lived vicariously through her successes. She also became aware of how she was creating the same dynamic with her oldest daughter. We realized that it was time to end this cycle.

As Faith grew, her dynamics with her children changed and her oldest daughter began her own therapy. Unfortunately, her husband was not similarly committed to changing and refused to begin couple's therapy. At this point, Faith acknowledged that she'd outgrown her old role in the marriage, and that her husband was not motivated or interested in working with her to repair the marriage. After several unmet ultimatums, she decided to separate. Today, while she says she doesn't enjoy being single, she focuses on strengthening herself and figuring out what she wants in her next relationship, rather than seeking a relationship simply to fill a void.

EXERCISE 1

What rituals do you engage in to separate your work life from your home life? How do you let go of the vicarious trauma from your job? Write down the strategies that you use. Add some new ones that you are willing to try. Journal about what boundaries you have in place so that you don't get overwhelmed by work.

EXERCISE 2

What are you willing to let go of? When I worked at a rehab center, we had all of the patients write down on pieces of paper what they would like to "get rid of," and then we had a bonfire where the patients threw their papers into the flames to symbolize destroying the negative aspect of their lives. What are you willing to throw into the flames? Is it your righteous rage, your inability to forgive, your arrogance, your depression? Write down whatever it is and then either symbolically or literally burn the paper.

EXERCISE 3

What characteristics do you want to hold on to? What do you truly love about yourself? Start by making a list. Even if it is a short list, it is a start. You will add to it over time when you become aware of good things to be proud of about yourself.

EXERCISE 4

Plan a date with yourself. Figure out where you want to go and what you want to explore. It could involve walking around an art museum, listening to a music performance, or exploring an outdoor farmer's market. It could be simple such as going to a coffee shop or eating at a restaurant. It should involve as many of your senses as possible and incorporate taking in beauty. The purpose of this date with yourself is to discover what you enjoy doing and what gives you inspiration. So often we live our lives trying to please our partners or satisfy our family members' needs. It is important to slow down and realize what provides you with joy. Afterward, write down some positive things you learned about yourself.

THE FUTURE

YOUR PATH IS BEAUTIFUL AND CROOKED. JUST AS IT SHOULD BE.

When I reflect back to growing up with my family, despite the fact that there were some small bumps in the road, I realize how truly fortunate I was. What I took away from my upbringing was a deep capacity to love. I believe that is what makes me effective as a therapist. It isn't necessarily any particular training I had or my doctoral degree.

So often, therapists believe that it is their clinical orientation that is the greatest factor in helping patients heal. It is not. It is bigger than that. It is their ability to love their patients—to hold them in high regard and root for their successes no matter what. I have truly adored being a part of my patients' journeys through the ups and downs on their Ferris wheels. Although their names, professions, and other identifying information were changed for confidentiality purposes, their pain was real. It has been one of the greatest blessings in my life to witness so much healing, transformation, and growth.

I've learned from my own trials and tribulations, as well as my patients', that our imperfections are what make us interesting. They create the narratives for our lives and keep our stories colorful as we grow. We don't have to create the perfect story; we can however, embrace the imperfect messiness we all have. There is meaning to be learned from what has gone wrong, as well as what has gone right, and how we made sense of the situation.

HONORING THE CRACKS

There is a recovery slogan that says, "Don't quit five minutes before the miracle." I interpret that to mean don't give up on yourself or your relationships too quickly. Recovery takes patience. So does healing. If you leave before doing the work of therapy and self-reflection, you won't be able to experience the magic of witnessing your relationship evolve. The evolving process may involve messiness, tears, or stretching yourself beyond your comfort zone. That is where the growth occurs.

Letting go of our expectations for perfection is a process not an event. It is made of a million little moments of choosing to be honest and vulnerable. It involves showing grace for yourself and your partner when you fall short. It is apologizing and trying to do better next time. It is displaying humility and humor instead of perfection.

There is honor in our imperfections. To quote the musician and poet Leonard Cohen, "Ring the bells that still can ring. Forget your perfect offering." He then describes "a crack in everything," and further explains that is "how the light gets in." Throughout this book I have used many song lyrics, movie scenes, and television dialogues to illustrate that throughout the pain of our relationships' imperfections, the story still goes on. So many people want to leave their romantic relationships after the disappointment creates a crack in their hearts. One beautiful aspect about the heart is that despite all of its cracks it keeps on beating.

ACKNOWLEDGEMENTS

In 2006, there was a movie called *Akeelah and the Bee* which told the story of a young girl who grew up in an impoverished neighborhood and overcame countless obstacles to make it to the Scripps National Spelling Bee. I loved this movie because it portrayed the power of community in accomplishing an overwhelming personal goal. To prepare for the spelling bee, Akeelah enlisted help from the people from her world. Everyone from her friends and family members to the local drug dealer quizzed her and believed in her ability to accomplish her goal. In writing this book, I have felt like Akeelah. I would never be able to write this book if it wasn't for my community's loving support.

First and foremost, this book would not exist if it weren't for my patients. Each clinical example is based on a true story from a patient or couple I have worked with over the past 30 years. Although I have changed the names, occupations, and other personal data for confidentiality purposes, the pain, triumphs, and tragedies are real. I am so grateful to be a witness as well as an agent for supporting their personal growth.

Second, like everything else in my life, this journey was encouraged and supported by my husband of over 25 years, Jeffrey Adam Nerenberg. He was my emotional support through my doctorate program, the impetus for starting my own private practice, and the person who said to me, "If you don't write your book when you are stuck at home during a pandemic, when are you ever going to write it?" He was my first proof-reader and my biggest fan. Also, he allowed me to share some of our personal stories and our own vulnerable moments for the sake of honesty and authenticity in my writing. I appreciate my true companion more every day as we continue to move mountains together in this world.

Third, my children mean everything to me. Amanda so generously allowed me to use her stories in order to illustrate the power that comes from transforming pain. Her own work ethic and dedication for always doing her best inspired me to give all that I could to this project. She is truly the kindest person I know. Marissa, after reading one of my earlier drafts, told me that I needed to use more of myself in my writing and to go a little deeper. I hope I have done this in ways that make her proud. I adore her sparkle and our spiritual connection. Finally, Justin, my son the warrior, displayed patience as he put up with me spending so much time writing and in my own head. His own empathy and sensitivity have made me more compassionate and changed how I see the world.

In looking at my professional inspiration, I need to acknowledge my dream team, the original Keystone staff of Camelot. Dr. Pannill Taylor, Bob Dilbeck, MSW, Jeannette Cutshaw, LMFT, and Bob German. We've been friends and colleagues for over 25 years. Our connection is spiritual and deep. Thanks for your suggestions and for reading my earlier drafts, and Bob, thanks for your Leonard Cohen quote.

I am also grateful for the therapeutic team at Dr. Alyson Nerenberg Psychology Associates. I am so fortunate to be surrounded by such good people: Jessica Feldman, MSW, Ray Salas, MHS/CC CADC, Katie Dixon, M.S. Ed., Angela Kanner, M.S. Ed., and Janine Grogan. I adore you all, even when you are frustrated with me for the overwhelming number of referrals, I kept sending your way during the pandemic. We've all been working together for many years now, and I realize that my business wouldn't be nearly as successful without you.

I also need to thank some of my favorite author friends in the self-help genre: Dr. Rob Weiss, Dr. Patrick Carnes, and Dr. Kenneth Adams. Thank you for teaching me that a good self-help book can change the world! Rob in particular, thank you for your tough love, literary connections, and for being my friend for the past 25 years. Thank you also for introducing me to Scott Brassart, editor extraordinaire. Scott, thank you for "getting me" from the beginning and understanding what this book was capable of being. Without your organization, I'd still be floundering! I'd also be remiss to not mention the brilliant Dr. Brian F. Shaw whose thorough read through contributed to making my book even better.

I am truly grateful to my publishing team at Tree of Life Press. Joy Stocke, thank you for living up to your name and providing honesty and integrity as we brought this book to life! I especially appreciate that you never put pressure on me and allowed me to maintain my own voice in this whole crazy publishing process. Additional "thank yous" go out to Raquel Pidal and V Allen for assistance with editing and Tim Ogline for putting up with my perfectionism as we worked to design a beautiful cover.

"I get by with a little help from my friends." A special thank you needs to go out to my crew: Dara Jeck, Lisa Lefkowitz, Michele Shubin, Paula Glazer, Rachel Cohen, Dr. Jackie Kaiser, Robin Morganstein, Nancy Fineman, Michele Kaufman, Dr. Karen Abrams, Jennifer Howie, Candy Adler, Dr. David Zweibeck, Jamie Joffe, and Michael Rosner. Between reading my earlier drafts or continuing to ask me about how the project was going and for listening attentively while I prattled on and on, I am grateful. Thanks for always having my back and believing in me.

I also can't neglect mentioning my Psychologist Squad: Dr. Ada Ponpipom Martini, Dr. Jeanne Stanley, Dr. Tracy Steen and Rev. Dr. Nadine Rosechild Sullivan. Since our first year of graduate school, Ada has been my "ride or die" maid of honor and voice of sanity. Additionally, for the past 15 years, Jeanne has been the person who I run everything by professionally and often personally. Her kindness, generosity, and competence are unparalleled. Tracy is one of my more recent psychologist friends but in the 5 years since we first met, I have been blown away by how helpful, giving and supportive she is. Nadine affirmed that this book needed to be written, and believed in my power to speak my truth. She is a valued spiritual advisor with a beautiful heart. It is a gift to have so many incredible women in the field believing in me.

A huge thank you also needs to go out to my angel squad: Lauren Kline, Daryl Hornik, and Lauren Albert. Not only are you my closest college friends who've been there for me for 30 years, but you are so much more. Lauren and Daryl when I told you I needed you, you came running. No questions asked. I will always love you with all my heart. Lauren Albert, I knew from the first moment I met you at college orientation that you would be a lifetime sister friend.

Additional gratitude goes out to my PR Queens Marika Flatt and Leslie Barrett, as well as my friends Sari Lifshitz and Brighid Flynn for publicizing the sacredness of this book.

A special mention goes to my in-laws, Andi and Aaron Nerenberg, for their warmness and continued support of my endeavors. Additionally, another shoutout goes to the Althschuler family.

Also, I have nothing but love for my brother, Dr. David Serota, who has overcome adversity and will one day make it to Mount Kilimanjaro. I appreciate your sweetness and our always supportive relationship. I wish only good things ahead for you and your whole family.

Lastly, I thank my parents, Shelly and Steve Serota, who have given me so much, from their encouragement of education to believing in the power of taking a risk. I credit them with teaching me how to love, and in the end that is what my private practice and this whole book are about.

ABOUT THE AUTHOR

Dr. Alyson Nerenberg is a licensed psychologist who has been counseling individuals, couples, and groups for the last 30 years. After earning her doctorate in clinical psychology from Widener University in Chester, PA in 1997, she spent 5 years as the clinical director of the Keystone Center Extended Care Unit, a nationally known, residential treatment program for healing from addictive behaviors and trauma. Additionally, she spent 5 years as a board member for the International Institute for Trauma and Addictions Professionals where she headed the supervision committee. She has supervised hundreds of therapists and lectured nationally on various topics including healing from trauma and addictions. Dr. Nerenberg has spent the last 20 years running her private practice, Dr. Alyson Nerenberg Psychology Associates, PC in Philadelphia, PA. She had been featured on MSNBC, ABC, CBS, FOX, A&E, and CN8. Although she has written chapters in various text books and professional journals, this is her first book. In addition to her professional accomplishments, Dr. Nerenberg is most proud of her family, including: her husband, Jeffrey; children, Amanda, Marissa, and Justin, and their white fluffy dog, Rosie.

BIBLIOGRAPHY

Rothstein, Arnold. *The Narcissistic Pursuit of Perfection*. London: Routledge, 1984.

American Psychiatric Association. *Diagnostic and Statistical Manual of Mental Disorders (DSM–5)*. Arlington, Virginia: APA, 2013.

Roddick, Marjie L. "Big T and Little t Trauma and How Your Body Reacts to It." *GoodTherapy Blog*, October 19, 2015. https://www.goodtherapy.org/blog/big-t-and-little-t-trauma-and-how-your-body-reacts-to-it-1019154

Bradshaw, John. *Healing the Shame that Binds You*. Boca Raton: Health Communications Incorporated, 1988.

Alcoholics Anonymous World Services, Inc. *Alcoholics Anonymous*, 4th ed. New York: Alcoholics Anonymous World Services, Inc, 2001.

Peter Chelsom, dir. *Shall We Dance?* 2004; New York: Miramax, 2005. DVD.

Kirshenbaum, Mira. *Too Good to Leave, Too Bad to Stay: A Step-by-Step Guide to Help You Decide Whether to Stay In or Get Out of Your Relationship*. New York: Plume, 1997.

Weiss, Robert. *Out of the Doghouse: A Step-by-Step Relationship-Saving Guide for Men Caught Cheating*. New York: Health Communications Inc., 2017.

The Grateful Dead. "Touch of Grey." By Jerry Garcia and Robert Hunter. Recorded January 1987. Track 1 on *In the Dark*. Arista Records, compact disc.

Gilbert, Elizabeth. "WISDOM & AGE & WOMEN." Elizabeth Gilbert (website). Published June 22, 2014. https://www.elizabethgilbert.com/wisdom-age-women-dear-ones-the-other-day-someone-asked-me-why-i-had-ded/

Karpman, Stephen B. *A Game Free Life: The definitive book on the Drama Triangle and Compassion Triangle*. San Francisco: Drama Triangle Publications,1968.

Luskin, Frederic. *Forgive for Good: A Proven Prescription for Health and Happiness*. San Francisco: HarperSanFrancisco, 2001.

M.J. Delaney, dir. *Ted Lasso*. Season 1, episode 9. "All Apologies." Aired September 25, 2021, on Apple TV+.

Smith, Jeremy Adam, ed., et al. *The Gratitude Project: How the Science of Thankfulness Can Rewire Our Brains for Resilience, Optimism, and the Greater Good*. Oakland: New Harbinger Publications, Inc., 2020.

Emmons, Robert. "Why Gratitude Is Good." *Greater Good Magazine*, November 16, 2010. https://greatergood.berkeley.edu/article/item/why_gratitude_is_good

Schafler, Katherine. "How to Change Your Life in One Second Flat." *Thrive Global*, November 7, 2017.

National Institutes of Health. "Social Media Use Associated with Depression in Young Adults According to New Research from the University of Pittsburgh School of Medicine." *Depression and Anxiety* (2021).

Hunt, Melissa G., Rachel Marx, Courtney Lipson, and Jordyn Young. "No more FOMO: Limiting social media decreases loneliness and depression." *Journal of Social and Clinical Psychology* 37, no. 10 (2018): 751-768.

Minuchin, Salvador. *Families and Family Therapy*. Cambridge: Harvard University Press, 1974.

Adams, Kenneth M. *Silently Seduced: When Parents Make Their Children Partners*, rev. ed. Boca Raton: Health Communications, Inc., 2011.

Adams, Kenneth M. and Alexander P. Morgan. *When He's Married to Mom: How to Help Mother-Enmeshed Men Open Their Hearts to True Love and Commitment*. New York: Touchstone, 2007.

Tate Taylor, dir. *The Help*. 2011; Glendale: DreamWorks, 2011. DVD.

Snowden, Kristin M. and Scott Brassart. *Life Anonymous: 12 Steps to Heal and Transform Your Life*. Self-published, 2020.

Cohan, Catherine L. and Steve W. Cole. "Life Course Transitions and Natural Disaster: Marriage, Birth, and Divorce Following Hurricane Hugo." *Journal of Family Psychology* 16, no. 1 (2002): 14–25.

Gottman, John M. *The Marriage Clinic: A Scientifically Based Marital Therapy*. New York: W.W. Norton & Company, 1999.

Boss, Pauline. *Ambiguous Loss: Learning to Live with Unresolved Grief*. Cambridge: Harvard University Press, 1999.

Kübler-Ross, Elizabeth. *On Death and Dying: What the Dying Have to Teach Doctors, Nurses, Clergy and Their Own Families*. New York: The Macmillan Company, 1969.

Martin Brest, dir. *Scent of a Woman*. 1992; New York: Universal Pictures, 1992. DVD.

Gus Van Sant, dir. *Good Will Hunting*. 1997; New York: Miramax, 1997. DVD.

Miller, Alice. *The Drama of the Gifted Child: The Search for the True Self*. Translated by Ruth Ward. New York: Basic Books, 1981.

Beatty, Melody. *Codependent No More: How to Stop Controlling Others and Start Caring for Yourself*. Center City: Hazelden, 1986.

Doug Atchison, dir. *Akeelah and the Bee*. 2006; Santa Monica: Lionsgate, 2006. DVD.